D0742390

F
O   COPY 1

O'DELL

THE FEATHERED SERPENT

F
O   O'DELL   COPY 1

THE FEATHERED SERPENT

THE
FEATHERED
SERPENT

Also by Scott O'Dell

THE BLACK PEARL

THE CAPTIVE

CARLOTA

CHILD OF FIRE

THE CRUISE OF THE ARCTIC STAR

THE DARK CANOE

THE HAWK THAT DARE NOT HUNT BY DAY

ISLAND OF THE BLUE DOLPHINS

JOURNEY TO JERICHO

KATHLEEN, PLEASE COME HOME

THE KING'S FIFTH

SARAH BISHOP

SING DOWN THE MOON

THE TREASURE OF TOPO-EL-BAMPO

THE 290

ZIA

THE
FEATHERED
SERPENT

Scott O'Dell

Houghton Mifflin Company
Boston 1981

Printed in the United States of America
10 9 8 7 6 5 4 3 2 1

Library of Congress Cataloging in Publication Data
O'Dell, Scott, 1903–
    The feathered serpent.

    Sequel to: The captive.
    Summary: A young Spanish seminarian who the Mayas
believe is their powerful god, Kukulcán, witnesses the
coming of Cortés and the capture of the magnificent
Aztec city, Tenochtitlán.
    [1. Mayas—Fiction. 2. Aztecs—Fiction. 3. Indians
of Mexico—Fiction. 4. Mexico—History—Conquest, 1519–
1540—Fiction] I. Title.
PZ7.0237Fe   [Fic]   81–7888
ISBN 0–395–30851–8   AACR2

Author's Note

The Feathered Serpent is the second book of a chronicle based upon the legend of Kukulcán, god of the Maya, who came to Yucatán in southeastern Mexico during the ninth century A.D. Kukulcán was not born a god but became one because of his humble and compassionate life. He ruled over the great nation of the Maya for several centuries, then mysteriously disappeared, promising to return.

In *The Captive,* the first book of this chronicle, a young Spanish seminarian is cast away among the Maya and by chance assumes the guise of Kukulcán.

The Feathered Serpent continues his story.

THE
FEATHERED
SERPENT

•

Once more, lest it be forgot, I swear in the name of the cock that crew for our holy apostle St. Peter, by the bronze horse of Toledo, by the six blind bishops of Valladolid, and now in the name of Kukulcán, Feathered Serpent, Lord of the Twilight. I swear that what I write here is the truth.

The mountain of St. John the Baptist was crested with snow, but out of its mouth still rose a ragged plume that the wind caught and spread across the jungle in a fiery mist.

A thousand canoes lay tethered along the sea wall. As many more rode at anchor in the calm waters of the bay. Some could be seen in the strait between the bay and the mainland cliffs.

Behind me rose the red stone walls of the godhouse.

Far below the terrace on which I stood, in the plaza at the base of the great temple, the multitude chanted my name. The chanting grew loud and faded away. The sweet smell of copal burning in a thousand braziers drifted upward. Conches wailed and drums beat.

1

Cantú, the dwarf, spoke something in my ear. It was lost in a sudden outburst from below as another, the fifty-first prisoner, was led forth.

The black-robed priests placed the victim upon the altar stone. They laid him down gently, as if he were a young and beloved brother, and held him there facing the murky sky. He was a mere boy, with thin wrists and ribs that showed through his skin. In his hair was a scarlet bloom.

The sacrificial priest came out of the shadows of the godhouse, grasping his obsidian knife. He plunged the knife into the boy's chest and quickly drew out his steaming heart. The sun was hidden, but he thrust the heart aloft toward the place the sun should be. Then he dropped it, still beating, in a votive vase among other hearts that had ceased to beat.

Four priests took the body from the altar stone. They tossed it down the steep flight of steps, toward the pile of bodies at the base of the temple. On its downward flight it lodged among the steps. Priestly ushers promptly rushed out and with a shove sent the body careening on its way.

The boy's lost flower lay behind on the terrace and I picked it up. It was like those I had seen months before, the morning I had landed on the island. Indeed, the first thing my eyes had met when I crawled out of the raging sea was a bed of these scarlet flowers growing among the grass. The one in my hand held the wild scent of that stormy day.

I glanced down at the temple steps. Some glistened freshly red, some showed brown where old blood had dried. Copal smoke tightened my throat, and the terrace began to tilt beneath my feet. The dwarf put out a hand to steady me.

"Let us go while the crowd still cheers," he shouted above the waves of sound. "For silence follows all cheering, even that which honors a god's return."

"Julián Escobar a god?" Unbelieving, I said the words aloud. "A god, the Feathered Serpent of the Maya!"

"Vámonos," the dwarf said and grasped my arm in his tight little fist. "Let us go."

I did not move.

I tried to shut out the monstrous sights around me. I gazed away from them at the sunless sky, the fiery mountain, the jungle and the sea and the far cliffs of the mainland. I tried to close my ears to the sound of chanting, the tormented drums and wailing conches. But the barbarous scene drew me back.

I caught the glance of Chalco, the high priest, standing beside the altar stone, with the obsidian knife in his hands.

Through slits in his jaguar mask he was watching me, his eyes cold and unmoving. They said to me, You are an emissary of a scheming king. You have come to our island city to do his evil will. For this reason, before the sun goes to its nightly rest the sacred knife will remove your heart, as you have seen the hearts of others removed.

It has been observed that in times of danger — as the sword descends, the wild beast springs, serpents poise to strike — at those perilous moments a man's whole life swiftly unwinds before him, like a thread from a spinning spool. This may be true, but *my* life did *not* unwind as I felt these threatening words.

Instead, the barbarous scene faded and for an instant I was again a castaway. I stood on the beach and watched while Don Guillermo Cantú, the dwarf who now crouched beside me, was lifted from his canoe by two strong Indians and deposited at my feet.

Once more I listened while, speaking in his high-pitched voice with the bearing of a Spanish *caballero,* he said, laying the plot that in a few days' time had brought me to this terrace where I now stood, "Your choice, *amigo,* is simple. You accept the role I have chosen for you, or you die."

I heard myself say to the assembly of priests from the back of my stallion, Bravo, speaking in what I knew of the Maya language, using the words the dwarf had given me, imposed upon me by threats of death, "I have come back after many years in eastern lands. I appear, as you can see and as I promised, in a different body, the body of a young man blue-eyed and white of skin. I come to rule this kingdom once again. My name is Kukulcán."

The beach, the flotilla of canoes that brought me to the city, my triumphal ride through the cheering crowds, all were gone. Once more I faced the high priest with his dripping knife and the phalanx of helpers in their black, blood-spattered gowns, ready and anxious to do his bidding.

Bravo was tethered behind the door of the godhouse, not ten paces away. I could mount the stallion and flee down the long corridors of the temple into the square, to the safety of the multitude that now chanted my name. I faced the high priest. I did not move. It was not courage that held me there, but the words of Cantú, the dwarf, when hours before we had first looked down upon the city from this pinnacle. "Together we will build a city grander by far than Ilium or Carthage. Grander than Rome in the days when Caesar ruled."

It was these ringing words that held me, that helped me face the high priest until he turned away and gave his stone knife to one of the acolytes. I raised my hands to the multitude. Solemnly I swore, speaking slowly and using Maya words.

"To all of you," I said, "to every man and woman and child among you, I will bring the word of God and the tender voice of Jesus Christ, His son. This I pledge."

My words hung in the smoky air. They did not reach the multitude. Only the priests heard them and they understood nothing of what I said.

The dwarf plucked at my sleeve again. "We leave, señor."

I followed him through the massive doors of the godhouse. The stallion shied as the door opened and he heard the sound of drums and conches and the cheering crowds. He was impossible to mount, so I took him firmly by the halter.

The dwarf lit a copal torch and led me down the same winding corridor up which we had climbed before. We came to the vault where skulls were stacked in white, endless rows, to the storehouse filled with skulls arranged neatly one beside the other.

On our way to the godhouse, when we had passed these cavernous rooms, in which no light shone save that

5

from Cantú's torch, I had thought little about them. But now that I had witnessed the slaying of more than fifty prisoners and realized that the skull of the young girl whose moans had hung in the air and the youth with the scarlet flower would be brought here, I stopped and called to the dwarf. He came hurrying back.

"Señor Cantú," I said, "my first command will close these vaults and seal them forever."

"In that case, mountains of skulls will accumulate," he replied. "They'll fill the city square and choke all the inhabitants."

"My next order will end the sacrifices. There'll be no need for storerooms."

The dwarf's lips closed in a tight little smile. "A rash thought. Remember that you're in no position to give orders that govern the very life of the city. Not yet."

He trotted off into the darkness and I followed close upon his heels. The air was stagnant with the gathered smell of centuries. Water dripped from overhead and lay in oily pools underfoot. A noisome creature, somewhat larger than a bat, flew past in the direction of the ossuaries, brushing my cheek.

I crossed myself, saying aloud, "O God of hope, fountain of all mercies."

The temple walls pressed upon me. From all sides I heard the scurrying of soft feet. Cantú's torch shone small and far beyond. Still praying, I followed its flickering light.

• •

We came to the door by which we had entered the temple a brief two hours ago, but Cantú set off in the opposite direction.

Anxious to be quit of the noisome dark, Bravo again snorted and set his feet. It took all of my strength to turn him about. By this time the dwarf had disappeared, except for a spark of greenish light no larger than a firefly.

The corridor continued for most of a furlong, rising and descending, often doubling back upon itself. Jagged stones had fallen from the roof and lay heaped in our path. The air was thin and choking dry. My feet sank into a powdery dust that must have gathered there for centuries, so deep that the stallion's hoofs made no sound.

I found the dwarf waiting at an arch whose lintels were carved with seven knotted serpents standing on their tails, with heads raised and mouths agape.

"Leave the horse behind," he said. "We have ladders to descend."

Reluctantly I grounded the reins. Unwillingly I followed Cantú through the arch into an empty room.

Plaster had fallen from the ceiling and lay scattered over the floor. In the center of the room was a small opening covered with planks which with some effort the dwarf slid aside. Holding the torch aloft, he stepped into the opening and descended a ladder, motioning me to follow.

Down three sets of ladders in a zigzag descent, well below the surface of the earth, we came to a second arch, smaller than the one above, guarded on both sides by stone jaguars. The torch shone through the opening. My eyes were blinded. The four walls squirmed with light, as did the floor beneath my feet.

"The crypt of an ancient lord," he said. "Who he was, I do not know. No matter. There it is in all its splendor."

He pointed toward a huge sarcophagus at the far end of the room. In front of it were two objects, one on either side, that seemed to be piles of rotting clothes. As I approached, I saw that beneath the clothes were bones, skeletons with spears clutched in their hands.

"Warriors," the dwarf said. "Put there alive to guard the dead lord on his journey."

Behind each guard crouched a stone jaguar, larger than life, with eyes that glittered red in the torchlight.

"The eyes are made of precious stones," Cantú said. "As are the spots. A fortune in gems."

The sarcophagus was sealed with a heavy lid. Across it was a band of glyphs. I managed to decipher one of the figures, the symbol for Pop, the first month of the year, and a bar and four dots above it, denoting the numeral nine. The year and the name of the lord lying there I could not read, though they were cleanly carved.

Cantú waved the torch above his head. "Gold," he said in a reverent tone. "The walls, the ceiling, the floor, all you see, even the sarcophagus, is gold, pure gold!"

His hushed voice reminded me of the *Santa Margarita*'s crew listening as we had sailed westward into the waters of New Spain, while their leader spoke of the treasures we were approaching. "The houses have gold floors and walls of gold, those of the poor as well as the rich. The streets and byways are paved with gold . . ." I also remembered my doubts that such treasures ever existed. And yet, at this moment, I stood in a room fashioned of gold, dazzled by its brilliance.

The dwarf touched the carved lid. "It is too heavy for my poor strength, alas. The both of us, perhaps, can pry it open."

I said nothing, revolted by the thought.

"There is no telling what lies beneath," he persisted. "What jewels — emeralds, rubies, jade, turquoise, pearls."

I turned away.

Abandoning his idea, he circled around and faced me, shining the torchlight over the room. "I have dug into the walls," he said, "all four of them. Do you know their thickness? No?" He held up a hand and separated his thumb from his index finger. "Two inches thick, at least. We are surrounded by a shipload of gold!"

As he glanced up at me, in awe of his own words, the silence was broken by the resounding boom of a drum, followed by a second boom and a third.

I was to learn later that it was the Maya way of denoting time. Their days, like ours, were divided into twenty-four hours. The drum, located in the godhouse, sounded six times during that period — at the rising of the star Venus, in midmorning, at high noon, in the middle of the afternoon, which was the present hour, at dusk, and at midnight.

The dwarf stirred himself. "I have proven to you that treasure abounds. But let us proceed. There is more."

We stumbled out of the crypt and into the corridor, where I retrieved the horse, and set off along a steep incline.

The last echoes of the temple drum died away. The torchlight now shone far ahead, then flickered and disappeared and shone again. A massive door rose suddenly out of the gloom. The dwarf stood knocking upon it with his feathered cane. It was slowly opened by two young men who at the sight of the cavorting horse turned and fled.

An abandoned garden lay before me. A weed-grown path led to an empty pool where a pack of hairless dogs, similar to those that had bothered me when I lived beside the volcano, sat watching us. Cats of every color peered out from rocky crevices.

A huge strangler tree shadowed the pool, its gnarled, gray roots, larger than my arm, looped along the ground like tentacles, as if to seek out something to grasp and throttle, be it stone or human.

Beyond the garden was a vast, weather-stained edifice built upon a rectangular platform twice my height. An open terrace that ran along its two sides was reached by a flight of stairs bordered by broken columns.

Trees pushed up wildly through the terrace stones and creepers climbed the walls, which once had been blood-red but over the centuries had faded to a sickly pink.

The dwarf dropped his torch. "The palace," he said.

"Palace?"

"Yours," he replied. "The palace you are to occupy."

There was a long silence while I tried to fit together the thoughts that crowded in upon me. From the strait when we had approached the harbor, during my triumphant ride through the streets, from the lofty terrace, I had formed the impression that it was a place of grandeur.

However, during our journey through the temple's endless corridors, strewn with rubble, alive with creeping vermin and birds of prey, I had been visited by second thoughts. Now, as I looked up at the ruined palace, these doubts overwhelmed me.

The dwarf was disappointed at my lack of enthusiasm.

Pointing toward the jungle that stood close at hand, he said, "If you look you'll see what seems to be a hill. If you look closer you will see that it is not a hill, but a mound. Then if you look closer yet, you will see at the top of the mound a glimmer of red."

"A roof," I said.

"The roof of a palace, perhaps. The palace that stands before you looked exactly the same, engulfed by bushes, trees, and countless creepers. Three days ago, after we had completed our bargain and I left you on the beach, I gathered a thousand farmers, more than a thousand. They toiled two days and two nights. They slashed and dug and burned. They removed a jungle that has grown here for three hundred years as you might remove the husk from a nut. There are a few trees left to be hauled away. Broken columns to replace, walls to plaster and paint. But these things will be taken care of in time."

Cantú paused, waiting for the praise that he felt was due. In truth, it was surely a prodigious feat that he and his workmen had accomplished. I told him so in fulsome phrases.

"Of course," he continued, "the interior of the palace is not commodious. Yet more so than the hut in which you have been living. We have hauled out the accumulated rubble of many centuries. Also, we have gotten rid of an army of rats, snakes, and tarantulas. Not to mention a swarm of coatimundis. That reminds me — you said today that you wished me to gather up your pet. Are you still of the same mind? Hundreds of these pests are running around here, as I have told you. About the girl, Ceela, and her grandfather and grandmother and the two aunts, do you still wish to send for them?"

Gazing up at the ruined palace, imagining what it must be like inside, I said, "Let us wait until things are settled."

Rain began to fall, large drops like musket shot that dug holes in the dust. But the dwarf made no move to seek shelter. He gathered his feathered cloak around him and again pointed toward the tower.

"Beyond that red roof," he said, "lie other mounds. They extend in a line for a distance of two leagues. In some of them we'll find the tombs of ancient lords untouched from ancient days to this, like the one you have just seen."

I was struck with the thought of a city smothered by trees.

What ancient people, what *antiguos,* had built the road of pure white stone that led from the harbor to the Temple of Kukulcán? Who had built the towering temple itself and the palace, as long and as wide as the great cathedral of Seville, and the edifices that lay beneath the mounds that stretched away for leagues into the blue jungle? And having built a beautiful city, why had they left it? And why had their descendants, the people who were now chanting my name, returned to live among the ruins?

"Tell me, Cantú, what you know about this city and its dwellers. I learned a little from my friend Ceela, but I must know more."

The dwarf was walking back and forth on his short legs. He was not interested in answering questions. Indeed, I doubt that he heard me. His gaze was fixed upon the red roof that could be seen jutting out above the trees.

"We need workmen to unearth these mounds," he said. "I used farmers to work on the palace. But they had to go back to their fields. We need prisoners. Slaves. A lot of them. A thousand!"

"Why not restore the temples that already have been unearthed?" I said. "The one we have just left, for instance, with its mountainous piles of rubble?"

"You don't understand. There's a surplus of temples.

One for every day of the month. I mean to tunnel into the mounds and locate the burial crypts. You've already seen what treasures are hidden in these secret chambers."

He removed his jaguar mask. There was a glint in his eyes that I was familiar with. It was the same hot glint that I had often seen in the eyes of Don Luis de Arroyo, Duke of Cantavara y Llorente. As well as in the ugly orbs of Baltasar Guzmán, whose bones now lay, picked clean by fish, in fathoms of the nearby sea.

"All we lack are workers," he said.

"To set them digging in the mounds like a flock of demented ferrets . . . ?"

The dwarf blinked. He stepped back as if I had struck him a blow on the head.

"The temples are sacred to the Indians," I said. "It is well enough to unearth them. And this we shall do. With God's help we will make them into Christian churches, beautiful to behold. But we will not rifle them for treasure. We are not grave robbers."

"Already, señor, you speak like the Lord Ruler himself."

"I *am* the Lord Ruler."

The dwarf gave me an injured look from his dark, yellow-flecked eyes, which were much too beautiful for a man.

"Not two hours ago," he said, "you stood upon the terrace trembling in your knees, fearful it would be discovered that you are Julián Escobar, a beardless seminarian from an obscure village in Spain. That in truth,

14

you are a common castaway from a wrecked ship, and not the returning god Kukulcán."

"My knees did not tremble two hours ago," I said. "And they do not tremble now."

The dwarf curled his upper lip, which was as thin as a line drawn with a fresh-cut pen. "Do we travel this road together," he asked, "or do you wish to travel it alone?"

I waited a few moments before answering, to give him a chance to listen again to the roars of the people. They were everywhere — on all sides of the temple, in the fields beyond the palace. Their voices rose on the wind and faded away and rose once more like waves crashing on the shore.

"Answer, *amigo*," he said impatiently. "Is it together or alone?"

"Together," I said. "But you will understand that it is I who am the god, not you."

Cantú rubbed his chin with his fat little fist. It seemed as if he was about to cry. I did not relent.

"On the beach three days ago you threw a saddle on my back as if I were a donkey, beat me with a stick, and now are riding me down a dangerous road. It is time for us to pause and remove the saddle."

A tear, round as a pearl, rolled down his cheek. I waited once more while the sound of the chanting came to us on the wind.

"And further, let me remind you again to address me by my proper name — Lord Kukulcán — and not by just anything that happens to come to mind, like *señor* or *amigo*."

More tears glistened in his beautiful eyes. I had the suspicion that this Cantú from the city of Seville could laugh or cry as he wished. Yet I hesitated to push him further.

"Tell me," I said, speaking of a matter that had long been with me, indeed since the day the caravel sank beneath the waves. "Do you think there's a chance we can float the *Santa Margarita?*"

The dwarf smiled, showing two perfect rows of small white teeth. "You told me this morning that the ship lies in about three fathoms of water?"

"More or less."

"How? In what position?"

"On her side. Her bow wedged between two arms of a reef."

"She's been down how long?"

"Four months and more."

"Then she's still sound. Our divers, who are experienced in diving for pearls, can dismantle the ship — decks and ribs and planking. Then we'll put her back together again on the beach."

"You're an engineer of great promise, señor."

The dwarf laughed, "He, he, he."

"This Luis de Arroyo," he said soberly, "this duke who owned the *Santa Margarita,* and settled over on the mainland in Tikan after the wreck, tell me more about him."

"I said that he is ruthless, a man without fear."

"Capable of fighting a war against us?"

"Fully capable."

"While you were living there on the beach, did you

see anyone nosing about the reef where the *Santa Margarita* went down?"

"Nobody."

"Did it surprise you that Don Luis de Arroyo never came back to investigate the wreck?"

"No, because I had no idea that he was still alive. He was clinging to a piece of timber, fighting for his life, when I saw him last."

"How much gunpowder will we find in the *Santa Margarita?*"

"Ten kegs at least."

"Sealed tight?"

"Sealed with tar, as tight as the kegs that drifted ashore. Some of the powder you used this morning when we landed."

"And cannon?"

"A dozen."

The dwarf laughed again and did his little dance.

I decided to say nothing to him of the treasure piled high in the sunken hold of the *Santa Margarita,* the tons of gold Don Luis de Arroyo had harvested by laying waste to the village on Isla del Oro, by killing scores of its people and enslaving the rest.

• • •

My first impression of the palace proved correct. After centuries of neglect it was, alas, in a ruinous state. Innumerable rooms opened into two long corridors that ended in a desolate garden where fountains once had played but now were silent. The throne room was in a separate wing, a vast, high-vaulted room whose stained walls and ceiling were covered with serpent figures, some erect, some coiled, all of them crowned with feathers, symbols of the god Kukulcán.

To enter this cavern I had to pass through a doorway fashioned in the shape of a yawning mouth, neither beast nor human, a mammoth fanged jaw painted red that might have been the entrance to hell itself. I was in the palace only one day before I had it torn down and had two wooden crosses erected in its place, one on each side of the wide doorway.

My chamber was large but bare, except for an elaborate stone bench and a sleeping mat. Its one small window looked upon a field knee-high in weeds. The stallion occupied the next two rooms to mine, one for a stall and one for grass. Guards were on hand to care for his needs.

My first meal was served by white-gowned women who appeared in relays, walking silently on bare feet, with eyes downcast and trays of food balanced on their heads.

Appearing from somewhere deep within the palace, they brought forth silver bowls heaped with pink frijoles and stacks of maize cakes, red yams, and vegetables I had never seen before, huge portions of steaming meats I did not recognize, a long, carved stick upon which were perched, as upon the limb of a tree, a row of small, roasted birds, trays of fruits, and a brown, frothy drink, of which the dwarf drank two full pitchers. I ate little.

That night I prayed on my knees for guidance. I walked the floors of the vast throne room. From the terrace I had heard the cries of the throng, proclaiming me Lord and Ruler of the Maya, Kukulcán, Kukulcán!

But whom did I rule? Whom besides the multitude that had left the temple square and now on this night still were chanting my name from the fields around the palace? Would I rule the lords and elders and the hundreds of priests? If so, how? Was my power endless or limited, religious or secular?

These questions were settled the following day.

At my request, the dwarf called together the Council of Elders. They came down the long passageway and into the throne room to the music of flutes, three small men in headdresses larger than they were, followed by a band of retainers.

They came forward, making gestures as if to kiss the

floor, and halted before me with downcast eyes. In hushed tones, placing their feathered canes — badges of authority — at my feet, they then stepped backward, making gestures of kissing the floor as they left.

The three old men did all this without a word and with a clear air of relief. They had quarreled for more than a year in an effort to find a successor to a dead king. The quarrel was over. Their pride preserved, they edged between the two crosses and retreated down the rubble-strewn hallway.

Prompted by Cantú, mounting the stallion, I followed them to the terrace and watched while they made ready to leave.

As they climbed into their litters, a mighty blast of gunpowder — set off by the dwarf to prove once again that it was the stallion speaking — shook the stones. It crumbled plaster from the face of the palace, toppled pedestals, sent rats and coatimundis scurrying.

The dwarf jumped with glee as the three elders were hastily borne away through a cloud of yellow dust.

"I have three beautiful canes carved with venomous snakes and festooned with the plumage of rare birds," I said. "But what is their use?"

"They are symbols of power. They are to be used to rule the city."

"How? What is to be done?"

"Do nothing . . ." The dwarf was about to address me as *hidalgo,* noble, then changed his mind and said, "Lord Serpent, affairs of the city such as the assessing of fines for misbehavior, the collection of taxes and of garbage, such things will be taken care of as in the past.

You will have nothing to do with these common matters. Dwell silently in your palace and give thought to the larger issues of which we have spoken."

Two days later I met with the three high priests.

I expected the support of Hexo and Xipan, who had accepted me at once, before I even came to the city. I also expected the enmity of Chalco, the Aztecatl, and I found it again, though he was most anxious to declare his own devotion, as well as that of his hundreds of followers who swarmed over the temple and through the streets in their black gowns, their black hair matted with the blood of those slain upon the sacrificial stones. Though he was most resolute in his promise that against all enemies, especially the Emperor Moctezuma and his many vassals, he would wait upon my command.

I had learned from the dwarf that Chalco was born in the province of Chalca, near the Aztéca capital, Tenochtitlán. It was rumored that he had insinuated himself into the Maya priesthood by a large payment of gold and further strengthened his position by marriage to the homely and only daughter of a powerful Maya lord.

The dwarf thought that he was a road weasel, a spy sent to the island by the Aztéca, to burrow into its core and thus be ready to deliver it to Moctezuma when the Emperor spoke the word.

The meeting went smoothly, save for a slight interruption just before the priests took their leave.

They had touched their heads to the floor and were backing away when Hexo let out a cry and rushed toward the bench I sat upon. Reaching down with a feathered cane, he prodded from beneath me a snake half the length of his arm, one of the deadly coral vipers, and ground it under foot.

There was general excitement and a search for its mate, since these jungle snakes were known to travel in pairs.

The only calm person in the room was Chalco, the Aztecatl. He paused and glanced up at me. In his eyes was the same look I had seen once before, when he stood on the terrace beside the sacrificial stone, obsidian knife in hand. And yet I felt sure that he had had nothing to do with the serpent that lay under my chair.

At the end of three days I had gained a fair idea of my powers, what I could expect from the Council of Elders and from the high priests and their retainers.

There were some fifty lords in the city, but from all that I could learn, they were interested in little else than gambling. Apparently they gambled on anything that struck their fancy — how much it would rain when it rained, how many pups would be born to one of their dogs, how many prisoners would be sacrificed on a given day, the outcome of a ball game. I need give no thought to them, at least for the moment.

I still had no real idea who Kukulcán was, what he had done while he lived on the island, his nature and ambitions. Since I was posing as Kukulcán and accepted as Kukulcán by the people, I could not go among them, or to the Council of Elders or to the priests, and say, "Who am I? What have I done? What is it that I should do?"

It occurred to me to seek my identity in the archives kept by the priests, and housed a short walk from the

22

palace. The building was squat and had a stubby tower from which the stars were watched and read. It was surrounded by a field of broken columns and stelae, but inside there was an attempt at order.

My presence caused much excitement among the archivists who were there to greet me, word of my coming having been passed along by the dwarf.

Xicalanco, a lean-jawed priest in charge of the archives, and his helpers lay face down on the terrace as I approached. It took the better part of a day to get them on their feet, to open doors that had been closed for many years, and to find the books that pertained to Lord Kukulcán.

Since I had never attempted to read more of the Maya language than the inscription on the tomb that Cantú had shown me and the glyphs scattered throughout the palace, it was necessary to ask for Xicalanco's help.

The archivist rummaged around in a dark cubbyhole and finally came out carrying two books covered with the dust of centuries. By now the sun was setting, so I asked him to bring them to the palace early the next day. While I was still eating breakfast, he came with five helpers, each carrying an armful of books.

"Where do you wish to begin, Lord of the Evening Star?" Xicalanco asked.

"Begin at the beginning," I said.

"When you came to the land of the Maya, Lord of the Night Wind, or when you came to the Island of the Seven Serpents?"

"To the island," I said. "That was in what year? My memory deserts me."

"There are signs," Xicalanco said, "that you first appeared in 4 Ahau 8 Cumhu, but it is only a rumor."

This Maya year, after some thought, I translated into the Christian year 3111 B.C. "The rumor is false," I said. "I would like true dates, not rumors. The date of my appearance is much later."

Xicalanco searched among the books laid out on the floor and handed one to me.

I handed it back, not wishing him to know that Kukulcán, god of the Maya, could not read the Maya glyphs. "You have a pleasant voice," I said. "I will listen."

The book was not in the form I was accustomed to. Though of the same size as those I had used at the seminary, its pages folded from side to side, like a screen, and opened one fold after the other until it was some ten feet in width, with ends glued to hardwood boards.

Xicalanco read in his deep-toned, pleasant voice.

I understood about half of what he read, enough to know that the account, covering the period from the year 800 after the birth of Christ to the year 910, was little more than a list of dates. The day, the month, the year that Kukulcán saved the maize harvest by bringing rain to parched fields; the night that his twin star shone bright in the heavens; the hour, the day, the month, the year he left the island and sailed on his snakeskin raft into the east.

The Maya were fascinated by dates. Time and the stars ruled their lives from minute to minute, from birth to death. They held them in thrall, as helpless as a serpent's cruel eye holds its prey.

In truth, I learned nothing from Xicalanco and his many books, although we spent more than a week going through them. They were beautiful works — the glyphs painted in bold hues on cream-colored paper of a high gloss — but they did not answer any of the questions that concerned me.

● ● ● ●

Could Ceela's grandfather, the old man who lived at the foot of the volcano, answer my questions? As a high priest Ah den Yaxche must have heard the legends about the young captain who came to the island from a far land, stayed among the people for centuries, taught them his ways, became a god, then mysteriously disappeared.

When Xicalanco gathered up his books after a futile hour of reading I turned to the dwarf. At the moment he was finishing his second helping of maize cakes and his third bowl of pink frijoles.

"Don Guillermo, today we send for Ah den Yaxche."

"Why, Lord Serpent?"

"Because I wish to talk to him. He knows who Kukulcán was, what he did while he was on this island, which I do not. Nor do you."

"Can you be certain that he won't repeat everything you ask him? He's an old man in his dotage. Can you trust him?"

"I trust myself."

"What if he refuses to come?"

"Bring him!"

"Today the pearl divers return from the south. I need to gather the crew we spoke about and make our plans for floating the ship. I'll go for the old man tomorrow, if it pleases you."

"It doesn't please me. Go today."

The dwarf went off whistling, a sign that he was in a bad mood. Late in the afternoon he returned with news that Ah den Yaxche was ill.

"Did you talk to him?" I asked.

"No, to the two aunts and the grandmother."

"To the granddaughter?"

"She was nowhere in sight."

Two days later I sent him back with an escort of palace guards. The following day I heard a commotion on the palace steps and, looking out, witnessed the arrival of the dwarf and curtained litters containing Ah den Yaxche, the women, and my friend Ceela.

I expected the old man to come forth, but the curtains remained closed until a guard flung them apart. Still he did not appear. His hands and feet, it turned out, had been tied with heavy cords. I ordered him unbound.

Confused, as well he might be, Ah den Yaxche stood stiffly gazing at his surroundings. For a moment I feared that he was about to take to his heels. I turned to his granddaughter for help, but Ceela lay mute, flat upon the terrace stones, her face covered. The others were huddled on their knees.

Overcoming the temptation to speak to the old man in a godlike manner, I apologized for the trouble I had caused. After some moments of hesitation, during which he again seemed to be at the point of running away, he gathered up the women and we all trooped inside, except for Ceela, who had to be carried.

The old man followed me into the throne room, but when I seated myself on the jaguar bench and bade him to make himself comfortable on the deerskins spread at my feet, he shook his head and continued to stand.

In no way did he fit the person I expected to meet. All of the Maya I had seen were short, not more than five feet in height, sturdily built, beardless, and bronze-skinned.

Ah den Yaxche was the opposite in every way. Dressed in a long white robe, he was taller than I, whip-thin, and pale. He was not tattooed or decorated with earrings and nose plug, and he wore a beard.

The beard stirred my memory. Somewhere in my studies I had seen a drawing of an Egyptian priest. He was tall, dressed in a long robe, like this man, and had the same small beard that curved outward and came to a point. The two men might have been brothers.

My guest stood in front of me and looked everywhere except in my direction. He was trying hard, I presumed, to swallow his ire at being snatched up, bound hand and foot, and carried off against his will to face a god unknown to him.

There was a long silence. The old man glanced toward

the windows, and again I feared that he was about to flee.

I offered him a bowl of fruit. He shook his head. I had not heard the man speak a word. Perhaps he could not speak. Perhaps he was mute. At least he could hear.

"You have been sick," I said, hoping to soften his anger. "I trust you are better."

The silence deepened. Just as I decided that he *was* mute, the old man cleared his throat and to my great surprise said, "I have not been sick."

To my further surprise, he spoke without a trace of anger and in the firm voice of a young man.

"If you were not sick," I said with some anger, "what in the name of Itzamná were you?"

"Confused in my thoughts," he said.

"Are you confused now?" I said. "I have questions to ask and I don't have the time to listen to confused answers."

"No longer," the old man said. "I did not want to talk to you while my thoughts were confused. Now my head is very clear."

He walked to a window and glanced out. Fog was slowly engulfing the city.

"I seek your advice," I said. "As you are a high priest, one who has seen life on this island, your answers should be helpful."

"Either of help or not of help," he answered, "my answers will be truthful."

"The truth is sometimes of help," I said, repeating rather pompously, I fear, advice given me long before by my teacher, Father Expoleta.

The old man looked at me for the first time. There was no sign of awe or reverence in his glance. It should have warned me of what was to come.

"Let us begin with the most important truth," he said, framing his words precisely, assuming that my knowledge of Maya was imperfect. "You are not the Feathered Serpent. Instead, young man, you are an impostor."

Pausing to gauge the effects of his words, the old man looked down upon me as a schoolmaster might confront a student who has committed some thoughtless prank. I returned his gaze resolutely, but inside, in the marrow of my bones, I flinched.

"Those are dangerous words," I wanted to say.

I could remind Ah den Yaxche, standing stiff and censorious in his long white robe, that I could have him seized, as he had been seized this very day, and placed in a cage with the rest of the prisoners, those who had not been sacrificed in my honor. There he would await the hour when he himself was laid out upon the stone and his heart removed.

These violent thoughts raced through my mind, but wisely I remained silent. I was moved by the man's courage. What did he hope to gain by speaking to me as an enemy? Nothing, I was certain, that was worth the loss of his life. Of course, what seemed like courage could also be the simple outpouring of an old man gone soft in the head.

I was calm, at least I tried to give this impression. I forced myself to smile. "You are a man of intelligence," I said. "You were once a high priest. How can you make this mistake?"

He did not answer, but went on looking down at me in a critical way, as if I were an unruly young man who needed a lecture he had not quite decided upon.

"How can you harbor any doubt?" I said, deciding that it might be wise to give him a quiet warning. "Such a doubt could cause you harm."

"There is not one doubt," he said, as if he had not heard me. "There are many. They go far back, to the day that my granddaughter saw the big canoe with the white wings sink beneath the waves. She brought the word. She saw you in the sea. She saw you lie on the shore. Not like a god, but like a dead man you lay on the shore."

"Gods," I said, "sometimes face adversity."

"They do not lie helpless like dead people until the sun warms their bones and brings them to life again."

Fog drifted into the room. The old man shivered and pulled the robe around his thin shoulders.

"Nor do gods sleep in hollow logs," he continued. "Without a fire, eating what they find in the sea and forest."

As he went on to describe the life I had led during my months on the beach, I recalled ancient gods who had met greater trials than mine — Prometheus, chained to a rock while a vulture pecked at his liver; Vulcan, whose father pushed him from heaven, who fell to Earth, taking a day to do so — but these gods Ah den Yaxche had never heard of.

The old man gave out a sigh. "Kukulcán did not live in this way," he said slowly, as if he spoke the words against his will. "He was not a vagabond."

"What was he, then?" I said, seizing the chance I had hoped for.

"He was a god."

"But what made him a god? What did he say? What did he do?"

I was afraid the old man would turn the questions back to me and say that since I presented myself as the god Kukulcán, I should know what made me a god and also what I said and did as a god, that I should not have to ask him.

He searched his memory for a long time, until I began to think that he had forgotten my questions.

"The Feathered Serpent came from the east," he said. "From where the sun rises. He came in a big canoe that was as big as this room and had turned-up ends. Or this is what I have heard from my father and he from his father, far back, far back."

I had read somewhere, or heard it spoken of, that in the days before Christ many boats had sailed out of the Mediterranean Sea through the Straits of Hercules and were seen no more. Could this man with his pointed beard, who looked like the drawing I once had seen of an Egyptian priest, be descended from these early voyagers?

"The Feathered Serpent went among the multitudes and talked words that they could understand," the old man said. "He talked also to the nobles and priests, in different words but words that meant the same."

Ah den Yaxche walked to the open window and glanced out. Again I was fearful that he would disappear. Then he turned away and slowly cast his eyes

31

about the room, at the broken stones of the floor and at the walls riven by the storms of many years.

It seemed that he had forgotten what we were talking about.

"What did Kukulcán say when he spoke to the people and the nobles?" I reminded him.

Gathering his thoughts, the old man said, "He spoke of many things. But chiefly he spoke against war and the taking of prisoners and the killing of prisoners. He was likewise against the killing of beasts and birds. He was against all killing."

"Kukulcán preached," I said, "but apparently no one listened, judging from what I see now."

"They listened. Everyone, even the nobles and priests. That was a time when there was much happiness on our island and the people built many temples. But then came the bad times, when the Feathered Serpent left and sailed to the east. When he was gone, the people slipped back into their old ways."

"Back to barbarism, where they are now. And this is why, centuries after he was gone, you gave up the priesthood and fled to the jungle to live on a poor *milpa* at the foot of a volcano."

"This is why," the old man said. "Yes."

"You turned your back on the city and disappeared." My anger was building again. "You have turned your back on me. You wouldn't be here now if I had not sent guards to haul you in."

"It took a long time to make up my mind," Ah den Yaxche said. "When I did make it up, when I decided that you were an adventurer and a common impostor, then I had another matter to decide."

He looked down at me like some ancient Egyptian judge.

"You are an impostor," he said, "but the people think otherwise. They have lived in fear. The city was seized by fear. There has been death in the streets and sadness in every house. You have changed this. You have brought happiness to the City of the Seven Serpents."

I had heard something like this already from Cantú the dwarf. But Cantú was a friend, whose life and fortunes were bound up with mine. At the moment Ah den Yaxche was neither a friend nor an enemy.

"What you are saying, old man, is that I am a god so long as you permit me to be. Unless I do as you wish, unless I follow your ideas about religious matters and affairs of the city, you will take it upon yourself to expose me."

"You put it in a crude way," he said. "I will not make suggestions that are unwise."

"Who is to judge whether they are wise or unwise?"

"You and I. We will judge."

"What if we disagree?"

"Why should we? Both of us desire the same thing."

"And what is that?" I asked, sensing our first disagreement.

"A happy place where people live in peace and love each other. As it was in the day when Lord Kukulcán ruled the city."

"The first thing, esteemed sir, is to have a city. Not what I find now — a place where buildings have fallen into ruins, the temple and streets are choked with rubble. We need to rebuild the city. And while we are rebuilding it we must find ways to protect it."

"From what?"

"From the horde that is ready to descend upon us."

"Of which you are the first?" Ah den Yaxche said, speaking in his young man's voice. "No, not the first. The first was Guillermo Cantú and his twenty-one companions. The twenty-one companions were sacrificed to the gods. Cantú was the only one left. But now there are two."

Cuidado, old man, be careful, was on my tongue to say, but I swallowed hard, saying as gently as I could, "And while the city is being reclaimed from the jungle I'll destroy the hellish altar stone and its bloody vases."

"This you cannot do and live," Yaxche said.

An echo of the dwarf's warning.

"And I'll also destroy the hellish beast and serpent idols that infest the temple. I will turn the temple into a place of worship of the one true god."

The old man cleared his throat. "I have heard of this god you speak about. My granddaughter, Ceela, has told me about this one. We both laughed. We laughed together. I laugh now at all this foolishness."

He towered above me, thin arms folded on his chest. He fixed me with a cold eye.

Wisps of fog, whiter than the smoke from the brazier, drifted through the window and settled between us. From the fields around the palace sounded the voices of a chanting multitude. From far off I heard the cries of circling geese.

Deeming it wise to have Ah den Yaxche located where he could be watched, since it was foolish to trust the old man, I found quarters for him that morning among the many rooms of the palace, placed guards at his door, and forbade him to leave the palace grounds. Ceela and the women were located nearby and given permission to come and go as they pleased.

A heavy fog billowed in from the sea while the dwarf and I were at supper that night. The windows being without glass or protection of any kind, the fog so filled the room that it was difficult for the servants to move about.

Torches were lit, yet ghostly voices spoke at your elbow, figures appeared, floated about, and vanished.

After supper I made my way to Bravo's stall to make sure that he had been fed and watered. I was returning when I ran squarely into a solid object.

At first I thought that it was one of the numerous stelae — the corridors were strewn with these stone markers. But as I reached out to recover myself I clutched a handful of wild, coarse hair. At the same instant I caught the pleasant odor of wood smoke and a scent that I had smelled before.

A cry of fear and surprise burst from the person I had stumbled upon. The cry was only three short words. *"Baax a kati?* What do you want?" But at once I recognized the voice of Ceela Yaxche.

A servant carrying a torch passed us and by its light the girl had a brief glimpse of my face. She opened her mouth to scream, then closed it.

"You're on your way to see Bravo," I said. I loosened my hold on her hair and grasped her hand. "Come. He's only a step from here. He's been fed, but you can feed him again — he's always hungry."

The girl opened her mouth. This time she screamed, just once, then, catching her breath, stumbled away among the fallen columns down the long corridor and disappeared.

Later that evening Ah den Yaxche and I discussed his granddaughter. He was worried that she would be unhappy in the palace. To ease his mind and my own, for I felt a strong attachment to this pagan girl, I talked to her the next morning. Or rather, I talked to him and he talked to her — and thus, in a roundabout way, we communicated with each other.

Ceela crouched on the floor behind the old man, who stood fanning himself with a small red fan made of parrot feathers. I could see only the vague outlines of her wild hair flying about, and her body stiff as if to defend herself.

"Is there anything I can say," I asked the old man, "that will calm your granddaughter?"

"Nothing," he said, "and it is better that she is struck mute by your presence and would faint in fear if you looked at her. Otherwise, you would have a young gabbler trailing you everywhere. With the young there is nothing between."

"Ask your granddaughter if she would like to go to the school here in the city. It is a school for the daughters of lords, so I am told, but I'll see that she studies there."

This information was passed on and after a time a reply came back in a small voice.

"What would I study?"

"Tell your granddaughter," I said, "that she can study sewing and cooking, things to do with the household."

There was a long silence and then, "I know these things, dear Grandfather, I do them every day. I could be a teacher in the school and teach these things to those who do not know about them."

"Ask her what she would like to study," I said to Ah den Yaxche.

The question was stated and wasn't answered for a time. Then from behind the screen came forth a torrent of words, most of which I did not understand.

"She says," the old man said, "that she would like to learn how to dance. And also to paint with a brush. And likewise to make rings out of gold and jade. And to sing. She believes she has a throat like a lark in the meadow. Or could have if she were taught. Which, having heard it many times, I doubt."

"I don't know about the painting," I said, "if it is taught in the lords' school or not."

"It is taught. But the art of gold and jade is not taught. This is done within a clan. This clan is jealous. It passes secrets from one to the other, in the family only. And there are no women in the clan, just men."

"Send word to the clan," I said, "that the Feathered Serpent wishes the art of gold and jade to be taught to Ceela Yaxche, and find out from your granddaughter when she wishes to begin the painting. She will make a fine painter."

Ceela did not wait for her grandfather to ask the question. She answered it immediately, but still speaking to him, not to me.

"Tomorrow," she said, "in the morning when the sun rises."

It occurred to me as I sat there that it would be sensible to have the Spanish language taught in the lords' school. The conquistadores within a year, two at the most, would make their appearance. If some of our people, the brightest, were able to talk to the Spaniards in their own tongue, it might prove helpful. But who would do the teaching? There were only two who spoke Spanish — the dwarf and myself.

"Your granddaughter," I said to Ah den Yaxche, "should have new clothes. She must not look like a village drab to the sons and daughters of the noble families. Children can be little snobs about clothes."

Ceela was not pleased with these words and didn't answer until prodded by her grandfather.

"You dragged me away in a hurry," she said with some spirit, "and my other dress was left behind."

There were three dressmakers in the city. I had them

summoned at once and they set to work taking measurements, showing different cloths and styles. Peasant girls wore the *kub,* a single piece of decorated cloth with a square-cut opening for the shoulders — the same style of dress as their noble sisters, but of coarse material. I saw to it that Ceela chose the best.

While this was taking place, disturbing news came from the road weasels who had been spying upon Tikan.

It was brought to me by the captain of the Maya army. The *nacom* was not much older than I; he had reached this pinnacle through his father, who had been the *nacom* before him. He was a vigorous youth, tattooed on both arms and legs, with a nose plug and a jade ring in one of his ears.

"Our weasels," he said, "arrived early this morning from Tikan. They report that the enemy has stored up hundreds of hornet nests and is now strengthening the walls and deepening the trenches that, except for the harbor, encircle the city."

"When do they plan an attack?"

"Not for a month," the *nacom* said. "Now the stars are unfavorable."

"Stars can mean nothing much to this Don Luis de Arroyo," the dwarf said to me.

"On the contrary," I said, recalling that many of his decisions were made by an astrologer, "he's a great believer in the stars."

"One way or the other, I think we should waste no time in floating the *Santa Margarita.*"

Nor did we. Early the next morning we left for the harbor, borne on litters with guards marching before us.

A litter as it bobs along one way and another is worse than the deck of a ship on a windy day. It is better to walk, but the dwarf felt that walking was unseemly for a god and for him as well.

A flotilla awaited us, each of the canoes filled with pearl divers. Most of the fog had blown away and white clouds cast shadows on the motionless waters of the strait, which were as transparent as air and the same blue color as the sky. The feathered tufts on the poles that marked the channel hung limp in the windless morning.

We arrived at the wreck of the *Santa Margarita* before noon. The tide was low, which gave us a good view of her through shallow water. She had shifted a little toward the stern since I had last seen her, because of the gold that was stored abaft of midships. Otherwise she looked the same.

Her bow still rested upon the reef, held there by coral, long and sharp as a spear, that had sliced through her bow. Her masts lay aslant the deck in a tangle of lines and rotted sails.

At the foot of the main ladder was the skeleton of Baltasar Guzmán — mossier now than it had been before, but upon its chest, held tight in a bony grasp, was the nugget.

The dwarf saw the glint of gold as soon as I did. He gasped and for a moment was unable to speak.

At last he whispered, "Moses in the high mountains," and turned to me, his voice rising. "You never spoke of this. Everything, but not of gold."

He then shouted to the pearl divers, calling one by name. When the young man swam over, he pointed to the skeleton lying there beneath us, with fish, like small pieces of rainbow, darting in and out of its ribs.

"Muzo, do you see the man?"

The Indian nodded.

"Bring the thing he holds so tightly to his chest."

The ship lay in some three fathoms of water and in less than a minute Muzo had reached the deck, made his way to the foot of the ladder, and stood beside the skeleton. He took hold of the nugget, tugged, but could not wrench it free. At last he broke off the hand bones at the wrist and came shooting up to toss them into our canoe.

The dwarf placed his foot on the hand, broke the nugget free, and held it up. It was half the size of an apple, with deep veins turned dark with verdigris, but the surface, worn clean by shifting sands, shone bright in the sun.

Cantú stood staring at the nugget, turning it over and over in his fist. Then he held it out, muttering that the treasure belonged to me. When I refused to take it, he quickly hid it away in his cloak — hid it from whom I do not know.

"I've been thinking," I said. "It may not be necessary to take the ship apart plank by plank. Perhaps the damage she suffered can be repaired. She carries a pump. I know because once I helped work it in a storm."

"Where would it be?"

"I last saw it in the bow."

The dwarf called to Muzo, who was resting in

his canoe, and told him to examine the hole in the bow and look for a pump, which I described as best I could.

The young diver was thin and small, but he had a powerful chest. He stood up in the canoe and began to breathe in great gulps of air, until his chest seemed twice its size. Then he let the air out with a long *whoosh*, taking the wind, it was called.

Muzo grasped a rope that was tied to his canoe and had a large stone fastened to one end. Holding the stone, he let himself over the side and sank fast to the ship's deck. We watched him descend the ladder and disappear.

"Some stay down four minutes," the dwarf said. "Muzo stays down five."

There was a tightening of the rope and Muzo's helper let out coil after coil, as the diver worked his way toward the bow of the caravel.

Fish began to dart about. A spotted shark cruised idly out of the hold. Sea dust glinted in the light.

I counted the seconds — one minute, two minutes, then three. The helper still let out coils of rope. He stopped and I counted another minute. There was a jerk on the rope and the helper began to pull in.

Muzo trudged up the ladder and stood on the deck. Dropping the stone, he shot to the surface, climbed into his canoe, and took a long breath.

"The hole is as big as this," he said, holding his hands spread apart. "I saw the thing you spoke of, the thing with the snout."

The dwarf laughed, "He, he," and would have burst

into his little dance had he been standing anywhere but in a canoe.

"The hole we can plug," I said. "If the pump works after all these months, we can pump the water."

"But first we should lighten the ship," the dwarf said. "Bring up the gold." He glanced in my direction. "Is there more?"

"Yes," I said, since it could be concealed no longer. "Tons of gold. You'll find some at the foot of the ladder."

"Bring it out," the dwarf shouted to the divers, holding up Guzmán's nugget for them to see. "All of it!"

Beyond the wreck clouds shadowed the strait and the island, but when the sun broke through I caught glimpses of the cove where I had lived after the *Santa Margarita* went down — the stretch of white beach, the rocky headland that loomed above it like a sentinel, the cross I had placed there, the clearing in the jungle where the statue of Ix Chel, the goddess of fertility, lay in ruins.

I imagined that everything was unchanged since the day I had destroyed it — the serpent's scaly jaws and forked tongue lay in the dust beside a small skull cradled in the mouth of a jaguar and a foot that ended in talons instead of toes. One breast was left of all the four, and atop the fragments lay the head of the goddess, her half-closed eyes peering out.

In patches of sunlight I made out the stream winding down from the forest, the meadow where the stallion had grazed, my hut standing high above the beach.

I imagined myself at the door looking in at the walls bright with the pictures Ceela had painted of the stallion running with her on his back under a blue sky among blue trees.

My fire beside the house would be dead now and the ashes scattered. The tracks of the coatimundi would show that he had come to the door and, finding no one, had left.

During my past weeks in the palace of Kukulcán, with the drums beating and the throngs chanting my name, I had wished sometimes in a weak moment to be back again in the quiet meadow, beside an open fire. But now, as I stood looking at the beach and the meadow and the thatched hut, thinking of my life there, I smiled to myself and never thought of it again.

●
▬▬▬

The gold came up from below piece by piece until the largest of the canoes was loaded to the gunwales.

Since it was close to midafternoon and nothing else had been done toward raising the ship, I sent divers down to salvage the pump. Would it work after months in the sea? Would the hose be long enough to reach into the hold? If not, how could it be lengthened?

We found it in good order, but the hose too short by

some thirty feet. Remembering that hollow-stemmed cane grew in a lagoon at the northern end of the cove, I sent men ashore to cut a bundle of stalks. While they were gone, divers went down and broke off the coral spear that had been driven into the ship's bow.

The men worked until dark at this task. They wished to go back to the city for the night, but to save time I had them camp on the beach and begin work again at dawn.

It took all that morning to cut the ship free. The hole that was left, however, was the size of a man's body. Not only the planking had been torn away, but also two of the oak ribs. The divers covered the hole with a patch twice its size, using mats fetched from my hut, plastered thick with pitch, and set down in a wooden frame.

Night fell as this work was finished, but, doubtful that the patch would withstand the tides, I had the men continue by torchlight.

During the time the work went on these Indians never looked at me, at least to my knowledge, never came within two arms' length. They acted, indeed, as if I were not in their midst, although they heard my instructions and obeyed them instantly. It was a strange feeling, this being alone, sealed off from people by a wall of silence.

The canes brought from the lagoon were fitted into the mouth of the hose, into each other, nine lengths of them, then wrapped tight with reeds and sealed with pitch. They reached well into the bilge at the deepest part of the hold.

The pump handle had room on each side for two workers. I thought about taking a place on the first shift to encourage the men, who now were tired. I thought better of it after an admonition from the dwarf. "It is hard work," he said, "and you'll sweat. Gods, you must remember, don't sweat."

We started the pump near midnight. One of the hatches leaked and we had to stop to caulk it again. The dwarf made himself a bed on the pile of gold and fell asleep. The men stretched out in their canoes, resting while they waited their turns. Torches shone on the sea and fish of every size, from fingerlings to sharks, swarmed around them.

Divers toiled in shifts. The pump coughed, groaned, and spewed a broken stream of water throughout the long night. The caravel rose slowly, first the stumps of her masts showing, then her rail and hatch covers.

Near midday she began to list from port to starboard, hung precariously as if she were bent upon sinking again, then with timbers creaking floated free. Standing atop his golden pyramid, the dwarf let out a sound much like a rooster's crow, scuttled up the ladder, paused to light a torch, and disappeared into the hold.

We met at the foot of the companionway, where Guzmán's bones were wedged.

The torch shone on a mound just beyond the companionway. It was as high as the dwarf's head and covered with seaweed. Small crabs, startled by the light, stared out at us from its crevices. It looked like a pile of stones placed there for ballast.

The torchlight caught glints of metal. The dwarf crept forward and parted the trailing weeds, then stood up and faced me.

"Jesú!" he whispered. "It's gold. Pieces larger than the melons of Estremadura."

He called the divers.

"If you remove the gold," I said, "which will require all our men for days, where do you store it?"

Cantú chewed on his knuckles. He wanted to take the treasure away, to handle it, to sit and contemplate it. He could not bear the thought of leaving the gold behind. I made up his mind for him. "Leave the gold," I said. "It will not wander away."

At the stern of the caravel were the remains of our horses. I counted nine carcasses, which meant that the only horse to survive the wreck was my stallion, Bravo. And that Don Luis was therefore on foot, without a mount.

While Cantú held his torch I counted the skeletons that lay heaped up against the stern bulkhead, as if all the men had tried to escape at once. The entire crew must have huddled there as the sea rushed in upon them, upon all those except Baltasar Guzmán.

The tide ran out. We waited until it ebbed. With help from the canoes, a slight breeze, and an incoming current, we steered the *Santa Margarita* ashore. Good fortune attending us, we careened her on a sandy part of the beach, the patched hole in a position where it could easily be reached. Since the hull lay on its side, at a slant too steep to work on, we had the patch unfastened so that the hole could be used as a quick way to come and go.

The skeletons were carried out. We buried them in a

common grave marked by ballast stone, and I commended their souls to God.

The powder kegs were found, eleven of them. One we opened, to learn with great relief that the seals had held and the powder was undamaged.

Cannon, steel armor, all the muskets were then brought out and set on the beach.

As night fell, fires were kindled and I climbed to the prow of the risen ship and sang the Salve Regina in Latin, then as best I could in Maya. The workers listened but their faces showed no trace of understanding.

Shortly before dawn we emptied the *Santa Margarita*'s capacious hold. We left the gold where it lay and Cantú posted guards over it.

When the sun rose in a blaze of sudden light a cry, a single Maya word, went up from the divers. They stood on the deck and each pricked his thumb with the sharp point of a thorn. As blood welled out, they held it high toward the sun.

This rite was not new to me; I had seen it practiced on Isla del Oro by the slaves of Don Luis de Arroyo. But to my surprise the dwarf brought forth a stingray spine and pricked his own thumb. He then handed the spine to me.

"The pain is small," he said.

The men were facing the sun with their hands held out, but their eyes were turned in my direction.

"You are not taking a vow," the dwarf said, a pinched smile on his lips. "You greet the sun after its long journey through the night and the gates of hell. It is exhausted and needs strength."

I hesitated, but only for a moment. I placed the yellow-tipped spine against my thumb and pressed hard upon it. Blood welled up and formed a bright drop that ran down my arm.

As I held it toward the rising sun, my thoughts were far away, on the work that the *Santa Margarita* still required, and the use I would put her to once she was ready to sail.

Most of the populace were farmers, tied to their farms. To fulfill my dream of the city that Cantú had envisioned as we stood on the terrace of the godhouse, I must gather from someplace an army of workers.

That place was in the hands of Don Luis de Arroyo.

God willing, with the use of the caravel and her cannon I would capture a thousand of his men, two thousand if luck favored, and put them to rebuilding the City of the Seven Serpents — its crumbling temples, the palace, the once magnificent Court of the Warriors, the archives — and to uncovering the great mounds that still lay hidden in the jungle.

But what of the temple, its bloody stones, the barbarous idols that stared out at me from every wall? The dwarf and Ah den Yaxche had warned against destroying them. Their warnings weighed heavily upon me.

I prayed for guidance as I faced the dawn, but my prayers rose on leaden wings. They did not leave the deck where I stood. They scarcely left my lips.

Ya! My mind burned with a clear vision. I could think of little else.

•• ————

On a running tide we floated the ship. Using twelve canoes with our strongest men at the paddles, favored by calm seas and a following wind, we towed her north along the coast and safely into harbor.

The next day woodcutters were sent out to cut timbers for those spars that needed to be replaced.

The sails were rotten, but from them we traced patterns that were used to lay out new ones. Since they were too large for the women to weave as they wove cloth for clothes, we had them make small squares that would be sewn together.

More than a hundred women were put to work at the task. The muscular young *nacom* had charge of the sail-making and he drove the weavers, setting them up in the city square where everyone could see if they worked or not.

Meanwhile, our road weasels returned from Tikan each day with reports that the enemy continued to gather war supplies, to strengthen its walls, and to deepen its trenches.

The elders recognized our danger, but the high priests were firmly set against an attack on the enemy until

Venus and the moon stood in a favorable position one to the other, and to the City of the Seven Serpents, which to them was the center of the universe.

Our island was in danger, but according to the stars that the priests studied from their high towers, an attack upon Tikan would be doomed unless we waited for a period of nineteen days. Both our priests and those of our enemy were Mayans. They would make the same calculations. The Tikans, therefore, would be waiting for this same time to pass before they set upon us.

I had learned from reading Caesar's *Gallic Wars,* and recalled at this moment, that the great captain considered the element of surpise his deadliest weapon. If I were to attack Tikan while they were waiting for the favorable time to fight, I reasoned, I might catch them off guard.

Moreover, if I did defeat them, it would be a step on the long road that lay before me. It would prove that the priests had been wrong in their readings. And if they were wrong once, they could be wrong again. If they were wrong often enough, then I might be able to put an end to this slavish superstition.

Ah den Yaxche attempted to discourage this idea.

"It would not be wise," the old man said while we were eating supper together the night of my return. "Elders and priests agree about nothing except one thing. The stars. They have been quarreling now for two long years, since Chalco appeared. They quarreled so bitterly over who should govern the island that it was possible for you to appear in our midst and be welcomed as a god."

The old man cannot have enjoyed being shut up in the palace, but he showed no signs of displeasure. Indeed, he seemed to enjoy his new role as adviser to a god. Perhaps he hoped to pay back his enemies for the injuries they had caused him.

"Do you believe that the stars speak to us?" I asked him. "My grandfather did. If the stars sent a bad message on the day he was to plant his wheat, he wouldn't leave the house. Nor, when the day came to harvest, would he go into the fields if the stars told him not to."

"When I was young," Ah den Yaxche said, "I studied the stars and was the best student in the school that taught this art. By diligence I became the best of all the scanners of the sky. In time, I became a high priest and nothing was undertaken anywhere on the island unless it was favored by what I found from my readings. Then catastrophes took place. I foretold a season of bounteous rains. The rains didn't come and the crops were lost. I foretold good weather for a fleet of pearlers that was venturing south to a pearling ground beyond Tikan. A storm came when the fleet was returning and not a canoe and not a man survived."

The memory choked off his words.

"That was when you quarreled with the priests?" I said.

"When I left the city and went to live by the volcano."

"But the stargazing goes on. The priests are against an attack on Tikan. They have consulted the stars and found them unfavorable. I have decided to challenge them."

"It will do no good," the old man said. "The skies will

fall around your ears and every star lie dead before the priestly scanners desert their towers."

I ignored the old man's warning. Supported by the dwarf and the muscular young *nacom,* who saw a chance to improve his fortunes by a bold venture against the enemy, I had the *nacom* call out all the soldiers he could muster.

The number came to nearly nine hundred men, a third of them experienced warriors. The rest were farmers taken from the countryside. The divers who had helped float the ship and thirty of the best canoemen formed our crew.

The army was assembled in five days. On the sixth day, against an outcry from the elders and priests, with her new sails fitted, the *Santa Margarita* left the harbor to the din of conch-shell trumpets and drums.

Our fleet followed, carrying the army and also, at the dwarf's suggestion, Bravo the stallion, safely stabled.

We proceeded south along the coast, keeping close to land, and at dusk anchored in the lee of the promontory and its cross.

The next day, without the canoes, we made a half-circuit of the island, turned back, and anchored for the night again behind the promontory.

At dawn, confident that the crew had the feel of the ship, I set a course for the mainland. With a fair wind we crossed the narrow strait and headed south toward Tikan.

Tunac-Eel, our navigator, broad-chested and a head taller than the usual Maya, had made many voyages in the big trading canoes, some to places as far away as three hundred leagues. To help him in his navigation, over the years he had tattooed on his back and arms and broad chest small charts of certain lagoons and inlets he had visited. In the crook of one arm was the harbor of Tikan.

He was accustomed, however, to sailing canoes that drew only two feet of water, so I made it known that the *Santa Margarita* had five times that draft and could not be handled in the same way.

Nonetheless, we did run aground, luckily on a sandbar at low tide, from which we escaped when the changing tide floated us free.

On the second evening we sighted Xe ah Xel headland, where we planned to meet the flotilla, which had gone on ahead. They were there waiting with their torches shining on the water, and the big war drums booming.

I knew little about battle tactics, all of it from my reading of Caesar's *Gallic Wars*.

I did remember that Caesar placed the greatest priority on moving his troops with planned surprise and quickly. The Maya, I gathered, were not concerned with either speed or surprise. They believed in letting the enemy know that they were present, ready to pounce, hoping that they would be frightened into retreat or surrender. But the soldiers of Tikan would be under the command of a captain long experienced in all the tactics of Spanish war, not an Indian cacique.

Since the port of Tikan lay less than two leagues south of the headland, I ordered the torches extinguished and the booming drums silenced. We doused the lights on the *Santa Margarita*. The caravel and the canoes lay in darkness, silent as serpents in the grass.

A soft night wind blew out from the jungle and the sea was calm.

Everything was in readiness. Moored fore and aft with light anchors and slipknots, the ship was able to move away at a moment's command. Her cannon were primed and set to fire from either port or starboard, from bow and stern. Her powder kegs were protected from rain by heavy mats of woven straw. Her crew stood alertly at their stations.

Everything was in readiness for battle except a battle plan.

Accordingly, soon after supper I called a council of war. We met in the cabin that once had belonged to Don Luis de Arroyo. The room was large, the width of the stern, but the bulwarks had not dried out yet and were badly warped. The stench of sea-muck fouled the air.

Five sat at the long table upon which Don Luis had eaten his meals and with his astrologer's help plotted our westward course across the Atlantic and into the waters of the Spanish Main. The five were Cantú the dwarf, the young *nacom,* and three of his officers. I stood at the head of the table, apart.

Cantú lit a torch, hung his cloak over the stern window to shade the light from those of the enemy who might be lurking in the jungle, and lit two bowls of copal incense. The heavy vapors smothered the dank sea smell.

At my bidding the *nacom* got to his feet. He was an awesome figure in his black paint, white, curling stripes, and jaguar mask with pointed teeth made of gold. And he spoke in awesome tones.

"Lord of the Evening, Mighty Serpent of the Skies, we capture everything that lives in Tikan," he said. "Men and women, children, the old. We leave nothing except the dogs — those that are too mangy to eat."

He uttered more threats against Tikan but sat down without suggesting a battle plan. I felt that out of deference and caution he was waiting upon me.

Cantú, though his experience in war was as limited as mine, presented an elaborate idea for battle. It had two parts — an attack both by land and by sea. The land attack involved my presence. I was to mount the stallion and at the right moment show myself before the enemy.

On the bulwark behind him was a copper shield ribbed with steel. "You will carry this," he said, lifting it down. "Astride Bravo, your blond hair flying in the wind, with the sun blazing upon sword and shield, you will strike terror in their souls!"

I listened to all this with some discomfort, surprised that he would ask me to risk my life when so much of his fortune hung upon my safety.

"Of course," he said quickly, taking note of my surprise, "the *nacom* will place a rank of his best warriors between you and the enemy. As you know, they have never seen a horse. When they lay eyes upon you and the prancing steed . . ." He paused to hold out a musket. "Fire this," he said. "They'll grovel in the dust."

The *nacom* objected to the dwarf's ideas when I explained them to him in Maya. He probably thought that if the enemy fell in the dust, then all that would be left to him was to go about and gather up the prisoners, an unheroic role for a warrior.

Now that someone else had spoken, he was willing to offer his own plan. It was more practical. He explained it after some urging as he strode back and forth in the narrow cabin, his anklets and amulets clanking in the quiet.

"Much depends on the news our three road weasels bring," he said. "And we should not move until we have this news. Tikan has planned war for many months. News about what they are doing has come to me every week. They have built a ditch around half of the city. It is three steps wide and the height of four men. The other half of the city is protected by a lagoon that can be waded at low tide. Only at low tide. All this we know. What we do not know is what they are doing at this moment. Are their warriors ready? Do they know that we sit here behind the headland of Xe ah Xel with nearly a thousand men and a big canoe that spits fire and round balls half as big as their heads?"

It was time for me to speak. But as a god with supernatural powers, who was supposed to know both the means and the end, I need not speak at all. It was my privilege to remain quiet. My one duty was to act.

The road weasels reached the ship within an hour. Carrying straw bundles, gnarled of hand and stooped, two of them looked like farmers on their way home after a long day in the fields.

The third spy had a small gray monkey sitting on one

shoulder and a green parrot on the other. He was posing as a *pplom,* a merchant, and was the leader of the three weasels.

"No one goes into Tikan or out of Tikan," he announced. "The gates are closed to travelers."

The monkey clapped its hands.

The *nacom* told the spy to take the monkey outside and leave it. When he came back he was asked about the closed gates.

"Do they know that we lie here at the headland of Xe ah Xel?" the *nacom* said.

The spy nodded. "I think so."

"Why?"

"Because of the closed gates."

"The gates are closed during the day sometimes. You have reported this before. Only last week."

"It is the first time that no one goes in or comes out."

"The gates are heavily guarded?"

"Heavily!"

"What do the guards say?"

"Tuux cahanech?"

"When they asked this, asked where you lived, what did you say?"

"I said I lived on the road."

"Returning," said the *nacom,* "when you reached the headland, as you looked down on the shore, did you see our canoes? Were there any signs that we lay here in the darkness?"

"No," said the weasel.

The green parrot ruffled its feathers and repeated the word.

"Did you hear sounds or see lights that would disclose the presence of our big canoe?"

"Nothing," the road weasel said.

The parrot repeated the word.

"But you think that the enemy knows we are here?"

"Yes," the road weasel said, "they know."

The parrot's green feathers shone like metal in the torchlight. Again it repeated the weasel's words, this time three times over.

"Then we should sail," the *nacom* said, striking the air with his fist. "We should sail at dawn."

"At dawn," the parrot echoed.

The *nacom* reached up and with one quick jerk wrung its neck.

The dwarf was for sailing at once, which was impractical, considering the untried crew and my own small knowledge of seamanship. But the *nacom* ordered half of the warriors, some five hundred men, to beach their canoes and set off toward Tikan, using a jungle trail that ran parallel to the coast.

They were to reach the walls of the city at dawn. When the *Santa Margarita* fired her first cannon, they were to attack the gates.

I cleared the cabin and lay down, but did not sleep. I tried to remember the details of Caesar's expedition against Britain. There were two of these campaigns, but they had gotten mixed up in my mind.

I remembered that on the second expedition he commanded five legions of foot soldiers and two thousand cavalry. On the first expedition his men were weighed down with a mass of armor and had to wade ashore in a heavy surf, then stand firm and fight at the same time.

Julius Caesar commanded some thirty-two thousand men. I had less than one thousand. He had two thousand horses and I had one. But his army was equipped only with swords, slings, and arrows, while I had muskets and gunpowder and cannon.

One thing I did remember clearly. It was his dictum: *celeritas,* swiftness and surprise, always!

● ● ●

We sailed shortly before dawn.

Wind and tide were against us, but we dared not wait, since our warriors would now be approaching the walls. With the help of our canoes we clawed our way off the shore and around the headland of Xe ah Xel.

The wind shifted and caught us astern, sending the caravel along at a goodly rate, somewhat faster than the canoes. I stood at the oak tiller with Tunac-Eel, our tattooed navigator, at my side.

Three hours after leaving the headland, we entered a broad estuary that soon narrowed and, in a series of bends and near loops, brought us into a small bay fringed by a stretch of yellow beach. Beyond the beach, on the crest of a shallow hill, rose the walls of Tikan. Enclosed by the walls were two temples facing each other, glittering red in the early sun.

The fleet of canoes caught up with us and we nosed into the bay, silent and scarcely moving. The city had just begun to stir. The plaza between the temples was deserted, but along the edge of the jungle smoke curled up from breakfast fires.

A woman was carrying a jar balanced on her head down a flight of stairs that led to the plaza. Four men were about to cast a net from the shore, swinging it between them, and singing in low voices.

At the moment our anchors struck the water, the fishermen cast their net and it went out in a wide circle and settled. They did not pull it in. At sight of the caravel they raised their hands and began to run. The woman dropped her jar and disappeared.

"We have surprised the lordly Tikans," the *nacom* shouted.

He stood beside me on the afterdeck, in a fresh coat of black soot and a hawk mask instead of the jaguar mask he had worn the night before. A vain young man, he wore a different nose plug, a different set of earrings, and gold anklets instead of silver.

"The city sleeps," he said.

Cantú the dwarf laughed. "He he, he. Shall we roust them out?"

"Now," said the *nacom*. "Without delay!"

We were moored broadside to the city, anchored fore

and aft, headed north the way we had come in, and attended by canoes that were ready to move us should the wind fail. The *nacom* raised his hand. On the deck below the gunners caught the sign.

Six cannon boomed, one after the other, each spaced at the slow count of ten, exactly as planned. There was a short silence. From afar I heard the screech of conch-shell horns.

"Our warriors are at the gates," the *nacom* said.

Through the swirling smoke I had followed the paths of the six cannonballs. All had landed in the plaza between the two temples, which were our targets.

As far as I could see they had done no damage, but this was of small importance. In the hearts of those who had heard nothing louder than the whine of arrows, the sudden, horrendous crash must have struck the utmost fear. I had once seen this fear, among the Indians of Isla del Oro when Don Luis had used his cannon, these very cannon, against them.

Across the water in Tikan, Don Luis by this time must have come awake and scrambled to his feet. He would have jumped into his clothes and buckled on his sword. Yes, his sword, because he would not have left it behind when he swam away from the wreck. It was a part of him, like an arm. He slept with it.

He would hurry into the street. At this moment, from some vantage point, he might be staring down at the *Santa Margarita*.

Was she, he would wonder, a phantom ship that had sailed out of a nightmare he had dreamed? Knuckling his eyes, he would stare at her until certain at last that she was not an apparition, but a real ship, a weathered, storm-beaten Spanish caravel.

I spoke to the *nacom*, who signaled the gunners. Six explosions rent the quiet. Six more cannonballs leaped over the bay into the city. One ball toppled the god-house from one of the temples. Another bounced off its blood-red walls.

On the wind, from beyond the glittering temples came the throb of many drums, the sounds of horns and musket fire, and above all the roar of voices rising and falling as our warriors fought at the city gates.

At the second round from our cannon, as shot struck and spun crazily away, a lone figure appeared in the plaza. He must have come from one of the temples, perhaps out of a secret door that opened from some underground passage.

He shaded his eyes against the sun. For a moment he gazed down at the caravel. Then he removed his headdress, tossed it on the stones, and started down a flight of stairs that led to the beach.

Since the man was some distance from me, I could not make out his features. But from his arrogant walk, which looked as if he were marching to a drum, I thought he must be Don Luis de Arroyo. I was certain of it when the sun flashed on the blade of a sword buckled at his waist.

He came to a terrace near the top of the stairs, a parapet guarded on each side by two stone figures, which I took to be crouching alligators.

Here he paused. Again he shaded his eyes against the sun and gazed down upon the caravel. He would miss the great Spanish crosses that once had covered the sails, for we had not had time to paint new ones. Yet he could not help but see, in Maya red across her bow, the name *Santa Margarita.*

Don Luis was still too far away for me to make out his features, but I imagined with what consternation and disbelief he now looked down upon the ship he once had owned.

He stood high above us, erect and unmoving, as if he were not the least disturbed by our presence, as if smoke from the cannon was not hanging in the air and there were no sounds of armies fighting, as if it were a peaceful morning and he had come out to look at the sea.

The dwarf was uneasy. "It's a ruse," he said. "A thousand warriors are behind him somewhere waiting for a signal to fall upon us."

"Twice a thousand," the *nacom* said.

"It's an old trick," said the dwarf. "As old as the Greeks."

The six cannon that faced the temples were loaded and primed. The ship was surrounded by a swarm of canoes manned by warriors armed with spears and heavy bows. We were prepared for any surprise.

Don Luis did not move from the parapet. He stood with his feet thrust apart, a hand on the hilt of his sword, as if he had gone as far as his Spanish pride would allow — not quite halfway.

On an impulse, I went to the main deck, where I ordered the cannoneer to hold our fire. Hearing my order, the two men followed me.

The *nacom* shook his head. "If you go onshore," he said gravely, "if you are captured, the battle is over. When the leader is taken prisoner and he no longer can command his warriors, this is the end. It is the custom in our land."

"The Feathered Serpent," Cantú said, turning on the *nacom*, "knows well that it's a Maya custom. I need not remind you that it was he who gave birth to it."

The *nacom* bowed and was silent at this rebuke.

The dwarf tried to press his sword into my hand. I refused it.

"Gods are brave by nature," he said, speaking in Spanish since the *nacom* was listening, "which is good, but they are also blessed with common sense. What do you gain by this foolish act?"

He was right, it *was* foolish to confront Don Luis in the midst of a battle that we had not yet won, to expose myself to an expert swordsman, to risk the chance of bringing defeat upon the army should I be killed. Or worse, to be captured by his cohorts, who were surely waiting only for his signal.

The dwarf was angry. "Is it pride that leads you into this trap?" he demanded. "Is it hatred of Don Luis de Arroyo? Is it a display of courage? Or is it something else? A wish, perhaps, to test a Christian truth?"

I did not answer, for it was all of these things and more.

The dwarf shook his head in disgust. "Then, Lord of the Northern Skies and Lord of Folly, may you go with God."

I spoke to the cannoneer. "Watch for a signal," I told him. "If I raise my hand, fire." To the *nacom* I said, "Have your warriors ready to attack."

Climbing down the ladder into the nearest canoe, I was rowed toward shore.

From the shadow of the canopy that stretched above my head I watched Don Luis. He did not move. He seemed to be enjoying the bright morning and his thoughts.

There were some twenty men at the paddles, all well armed. However, before we reached the shore, I instructed them not to follow me, yet to be ready should the need arise. Not waiting to be carried, I waded ashore and started up the winding stairs.

I greeted Don Luis in Maya.

He replied in the same language, in such a bad accent that I had much difficulty understanding him. I did understand that he had no idea that he was speaking to the god Kukulcán, for he addressed me as an enemy captain, curtly but with respect.

There was no reason why he should recognize me. According to our weasels, the people of Tikan knew nothing about the return of the god Kukulcán. If they did know, then being Mayan themselves they would never march against me. Nor did they know about the raising of the *Santa Margarita;* our spies attested to this.

Don Luis had changed little in the months since I had seen him last. He squinted, raising an eyebrow, and smiled. He could smile and thrust a blade into your side, both at the same time, as I have noted before.

The sun was hot. He wiped his face with the back of a

hand and turned toward the west, where the sounds of fighting now seemed closer.

"You are losing the battle," I said, saying the words slowly, again in Maya.

He turned his back upon the sounds. He fixed his eyes upon my mask and headdress. We stood confronting each other in silence.

I heard musket fire. Then the warriors swarming around the ship set up an angry chant. There was still no sign that he knew who I was.

I repeated my words, holding out my hand to accept his sword.

His manner changed. His shoulders stiffened. His grip tightened on the sword. It was the same sword that his father had owned, the one I had often seen before. He would rather part with his life than with this weapon. I could see him swimming away from the wreck with it buckled to his side, floundering along because it was heavy, yet not giving it up to the waves. He would not give it up now or ever, not willingly.

"Don Luis de Arroyo," I said, speaking in Spanish, in the rolling accent of a Sevillano, "either you surrender or I give the signal for the hundreds of warriors you see on the ship and in the canoes to come ashore. We have, as you well know, a dozen cannon and an ample supply of powder. My soldiers are at your gates this moment. Many are armed with Spanish muskets."

Don Luis heard my words without changing his expression. He still did not seem to know that behind the feathered mask was an old enemy.

Yet something must have stirred his memory — my

height, my voice, the accent of Seville. For I noticed that as I spoke he took a firmer grip on the sword.

The warriors waiting in the canoes kept up their angry chant. The fighting at the gates had grown louder. Don Luis looked at me steadily, holding fast to his sword. Now was the moment for him to use it and thus, by the rites of Maya warfare, end the battle.

Clammy fear seized me. I was tempted to give the signal that would send a volley of shot crashing down upon the temples and hundreds of warriors storming into the streets.

I glanced at the caravel. I could see the gun ports, the black maws of the cannon leveled upon the city. The cannoneer would be standing ready. Nearby the *nacom* and Cantú, the dwarf, were waiting for my signal.

Don Luis gripped his sword. Something held him back. It was not fear, because he was fearless. Nor was it any feeling of concern for my life, because he had no conscience about such matters.

"What lies beneath the mask?" he said, speaking in tones he commonly used with servants. "What do you hide under the feathers, señor?"

My moment of panic passed. I turned my back upon the caravel and faced him.

"We are Spaniards," he said, "not savages. Let us talk together like Spaniards. The fighting at the gates will continue while we talk. And for many days, if I choose, since I have a large army and many reserves."

As he spoke, a loud, angry buzzing started up behind us, a sound that I had heard several times while I stood there. The buzzing grew louder for a few moments. Then two small clouds rose up from somewhere, apparently out of a hole, and swept past us toward the sea.

"You may have a large army," I said, "but they fight with clubs and hornets." A third angry cloud hovered over us as I spoke. "You can't win a battle with insects," I said.

Don Luis smiled but did not answer.

●●●●

It seemed impossible that at this moment he was not suspicious, for I stood not two paces away, towering over him by a head, a young Spaniard with a metal crucifix around his neck.

And yet I, Julián Escobar, once a worker in his vineyards, musician and seminarian who had followed him blindly to the New World, must have been the farthest from his mind.

Surely he thought that I had long been dead, drowned with the rest of the crew, my bones picked clean. For when I took off the serpent mask and dropped it on the stones between us he uttered a cry of surprise and hor-

ror, as if a watery ghost had risen up from the wreck of
the *Santa Margarita* to question him about his crimes
against God.

Since he stood open-mouthed staring at me, I broke
the silence.

There was no time to recount what had happened
from the day we had parted in the storm. And there was
no reason to do so. He would believe nothing of what I
told him, and certainly not that at this moment he was in
the presence of the Feathered Serpent, the god Kukulcán.

"Call off your warriors," I said. "I have an army at
your gates, as you can hear, and another army waiting in
the harbor, as you can see. The *Santa Margarita* you
know well from other days — the powder she carries
and the cannon she mounts."

His mouth closed at the sound of the name *Santa
Margarita*. His whole manner changed. He took his
hand from the sword and for a moment seemed about to
clasp me in a tight *embrazo*. He glanced toward the ship.
"The gold?" he stammered. "Is it safe?"

"Safe. In the hold, where you left it," I said.

"A miracle," he said and laughed, acting as if we were
seated comfortably at a table somewhere, not standing
on a battlement with fighting behind us and an armed
ship riding at anchor.

The sounds had grown louder. They came now from
streets just beyond the temples, not more than half a
league away.

"Call an end to the fighting," I said. "My warriors

have breached the walls. The *Santa Margarita* has her cannon trained on the city. You have lost the battle."

"On the contrary, señor, it's just beginning. I have a horde of warriors in reserve, waiting to surround you. I'll block the mouth of the estuary with a hundred canoes so you can't reach the sea. I'll capture the *Santa Margarita* and slaughter your army, every one, if need be."

He paused, fingered the hilt of his sword for a moment, and then gave me a friendly glance.

"But there is no need for this," he said. "I don't know what your position may be in the place you come from. But whatever it is, señor, it's temporary, as is mine. We are the first small wave of a tide that will soon engulf this savage world. It behooves us both to give careful thought to our fortunes. The conquistadores who will descend upon us by the hundreds, by the thousands, will not look kindly upon us, their brothers, who go about dressed in rings, anklets, masks, and feathers. We'll be killed or driven into the jungle to die slowly in any number of ways."

The sounds of fighting abruptly ended. A band of warriors appeared on the terrace of the temple our cannon had not hit. Don Luis glanced up at them and then at me.

"There are more where they came from," he said. "But why should I call upon them when we can settle matters between us? Forget what has happened in the past. Working together we can accomplish wonders. We'll join our two towns, which now are weak, into one powerful city. We will ask the King for all necessary titles. When the flood of conquistadores descends upon us, we'll greet them not as savages dressed in paint and feathers, but as Spanish gentlemen, proprietors of a thriving empire, duly blessed by governor and king, under the banner of God."

The fighting had not started again. More warriors came out and stood on the terrace. I heard the cry of a conch-shell horn. In the silence that followed there drifted up to me from the caravel a neigh, twice repeated.

Don Luis turned pale. "Bravo?" he said. I nodded. "Thanks to God!"

He crossed himself and stood quiet, waiting for the stallion to neigh again. I think that he loved this animal more than anything in the world, next to his Toledo sword.

The warriors who had gathered on the terrace — there were several hundred by now — began to chant, one word over and over. The word had a warlike sound, but I could not tell what it meant.

I glanced at Don Luis. He was no longer thinking about the stallion. He, too, was listening to the chant. I had a strong urge to raise my hand and signal the *nacom* to unloose our cannon.

Don Luis went on about the miracle we would perform together, talking in his most gentlemanly voice, with an eye on the warriors who stood above us. Then there came from somewhere beyond the plaza the screech of conch-shell trumpets. This was followed by the beat of drums. Suddenly, from between the two temples, a phalanx of Tikan warriors came into view.

They swarmed out of the morning shadows, marching slowly. They came to the center of the plaza and stopped. Those on the terrace descended the long flight of stairs. Together they crossed the plaza and moved in my direction.

There was not a sound except the shuffle of sandaled feet. The silence was menacing. I turned and glanced down at the caravel with its cannon trained on the city, at the warriors waiting on the shore.

Don Luis had always had a habit of drawing his lips together when he was about to issue a command. He pursed them now and said, speaking in the formal tone he used with inferiors, 'Señor Escobar, late citizen of the village of Arroyo in the Spanish province of Andalusia . . .''

His words were lost in a blare of trumpets that came from somewhere beyond the glittering temples.

The warriors were still advancing toward me. They walked slowly, shoulder to shoulder, less than a dozen men, though they seemed like a thousand in their armor of quilted cotton, carrying tortoise shields and obsidian clubs.

They came to the edge of the terrace and stopped, not ten paces away.

Here they dropped their weapons and bowed, touching their foreheads to the stones, and spoke my name in hushed voices, over and over. From our warriors they had somehow learned of my presence. The God of the Evening Star and the Four Directions, Kukulcán himself, stood before them.

73

Trumpets blared again. Black-painted warriors surged out of the secret passageways where they had been hidden. They began to chant to the beat of wooden drums.

Don Luis glanced at his kneeling warriors, then at the caravel and the fleet of canoes. At last he looked at me. There was no sign of fear or surprise in his gaze. At that moment I doubt that he had the least idea of what was taking place. I doubt that he had ever heard the name Kukulcán.

"Don Luis Arroyo," I said, speaking in a voice that I did not recognize as wholly mine, a tone that had come upon me of late, "You are in the presence of a god, the Maya god Kukulcán. It is customary to bow and touch your forehead to the earth, to rise, and as you do so, to lower your eyes in reverence."

Don Luis blinked. He tried to smile. He raised his sword and glanced at its shining blade. Again he tried to smile.

"It may be difficult for you to understand what has happened," I said, "and I haven't the time to explain. Someday I shall, perhaps. Meanwhile, fall to your knees, as you have seen your warriors do, as you have often done when paying your respect to the emperor, King Carlos."

Don Luis glanced away. His jaws tightened.

Speaking in a quieter voice, I repeated my command, adding, "And press your forehead to the stones."

He took a last glance at the square, which was now filled with a chanting crowd, at his warriors bowing in front of me, repeating my name. Slowly he got to his knees.

It was only for an instant that he stayed there — he barely touched the stones — and he did not touch his forehead, but I said nothing more. Nor did I think of demanding his sword, for I knew that he would rather die than relinquish it.

I felt no elation as I watched Don Luis get to his knees in what to him was an act of utter humiliation. It gave me not the smallest pleasure to see his stiff back bent low at my command. My only feeling was one of sudden power.

The young *nacom,* in a conquering mood, wished to carry out his threat to leave no one in the city, men or women, the young or the old, and none of the dogs except those not worth eating.

Against his wishes I decided to take only the able-bodied. I left most of the farmers and all of the priests, who, like our own, wore stinking gowns, stiff with dried blood.

I had a twinge of conscience at this number — some

twelve hundred in all — but it quickly disappeared when I remembered from my readings in Caesar that the great general, after a battle with the Atuatoc on the banks of the Rhine, had sold the inhabitants of their village, fifty-three thousand men, women, and children, into slavery.

The hostages were loaded into their own canoes and sent off, guarded by our fleet. At dusk the caravel followed in their wake.

Don Luis was scarcely aboard the *Santa Margarita* when he asked about the gold — he spoke of it as *our* gold.

I led him below, past the treasure he had wrested from the Indians of Isla del Oro. He picked up a nugget, and hefted it for weight.

"We must weigh this mass," he said, "down to the last ounce, and keep a strict record of it. The King demands his fifth, *la quinta*. Since the crew has perished, we'll divide the rest, half to you and half to me. A generous accounting, is it not, señor?"

I made no reply. Instead, I led him forward into the bow of the ship and showed him to his quarters, a triangular cubbyhole squeezed tight between the bulwarks, lit by a cloudy window.

He gazed around in disbelief. "This is a hole," he said. "No light, a horrible stench, and the bilge. Look!" He was standing in water up to his ankles. "What's happened to my cabin?"

"It's occupied."

"Occupied? Of course, I should have known."

I marveled at his arrogance. It seemed to have

increased since the moment he had accepted defeat. Strolling to the window, he wiped it with his hand and turned to face me in the dim light.

"Are you not uncomfortable in this new guise?" he said, disdainfully. "You're a young man of simple heart. You have simple tastes. You were, when last I saw you, a follower of sweet St. Francis, who gave his clothes to the poor and talked to the flowers in the fields and the small birds in the apple trees. Tell me, señor, how do you feel going about in a mask and feathers, with Indians kissing the stones at your feet, calling you lord of this and that? Answer me, does it not imperil your Christian heart? Does it not bother your Spanish sensibilities? At times, señor, do you not feel silly?"

My answer was not delayed. "Not silly, Don Luis. In truth, at times I have a strong feeling of omnipotence and this is one of the times. If there were a dungeon handy, I would clap you into it. This cubbyhole, I regret, will have to serve in its place."

"I can't breathe foul air and stand in bilge water," he complained.

"Try," I said. "This is the closet your slaves lived in — thirty of them. They lived here for many days until the night when they could stand their misery no longer and climbed to the deck and flung themselves into the sea."

I closed the door upon him with the hope that he would have time to examine his conscience, though I knew full well that he possessed none.

We arrived the next day at dusk to find a throng gathered at the sea wall and bonfires burning in the streets, word of our victory having reached the city by canoe and fast runners.

Subdued not at all by his hours in the dank cubbyhole, Don Luis demanded that as warlord of a sovereign country he should be permitted to ride ashore seated upon his stallion.

"I lack spurs and a proper Spanish saddle," he said, "but I'll not require them."

Nor would he, being a horseman of exceptional skill. However, I did not give him the chance to display it. Mounting Bravo, I led the procession through the firelit streets, followed by Don Luis on foot, a cohort of his warriors, and a long line of hostages.

The dwarf had gone ahead with a squad of cannoneers, and upon reaching the plaza, which was filled with a cheering crowd, I was greeted by a round from our lombards.

Still believing that this thunderous sound was the voice of the stallion, the people fell silent. But not for long. As soon as I passed, they set up an unearthly din that lasted through the night and beyond.

"They have had little to celebrate," Ah den Yaxche said the next morning as we sat down at the breakfast table.

A crowd had gathered in the meadow not far from the palace and were beating wooden drums. The old man raised his voice above the roar.

"Not since the raiders from Cempoala were turned back has there been such a time. But then only sixty-one prisoners were taken. A small victory. Most were sacrificed when you became the god Kukulcán."

"I remember the day," I said. "It shall never be forgotten."

"Now you have twelve hundred prisoners to think about."

"Not to sacrifice."

"The people will demand it."

"I intend to put them to work in this ruinous city of rubble."

"Long ago, fifty *katuns* ago," Ah den Yaxche said, one *katun* being the Maya number for twenty years, "the city flourished and was great in the world. It has lain in ruins for a long time. You cannot put it back the way it was in one day or in two. You will be forced to sacrifice most of the prisoners."

"Old man, honorable sire, we shall see."

Flushed by my success at Tikan, I spoke in full confidence that I would send only a token number to the sacrificial stone, a dozen perhaps, no more. I did not count upon the forces ranged against me.

I saw that the prisoners were rested for a day, fed well, and though kept in a stockade, had a warm place to sleep.

The *bacab* in charge of the city streets, Lord Xacanatzin, was given instructions to divide them into two working squads and to put one at work cleaning up the plaza and the Temple of Kukulcán. The second squad was sent to the palace to store away the stones that littered the corridors and throne room.

I found an artist in this group, a man who had spent his life painting animal life on vases he sold in the market. He was put to work painting out the mural that

79

filled one end of the room — a horrible scene of the two-headed earth goddess, with arms shaped like serpents and a feathered skirt embroidered with skulls.

Remembering that Ceela Yaxche possessed a modest talent as an artist, I called upon her to assist him.

Since she was familiar with the cross I had built, I instructed her to limn, as best she could, a picture of the scene around it, including the rocky headland, the sea stretching off into the distance, and the cross itself under a sunny sky, dominating all with its message of redemption.

She had already started in the school for nobles, studying ritual dance, cultivation of the speaking and singing voice, and the painting of glyphs. The class in Spanish was delayed because the dwarf had been occupied with the *Santa Margarita* and the war against Tikan. Now that he was free of these responsibilities, he had new ones — conveying my messages to the *bacab*, Xacanatzin, and seeing that they were carried out.

Believing strongly in the value of Spanish to the children of noble families, I called upon Don Luis de Arroyo to take over the role of teacher.

Don Luis was not pleased to be teaching a roomful of girls and boys (this was the first time that the school had allowed males and females to study in the same room), but he preferred it to spending his days behind wooden bars.

He was brought to the palace each day under guard, spent two hours teaching, and then was returned to his cage. I saw nothing of him during the first week of the class, though he made several attempts to arrange a meeting. Nor did I encounter Ceela Yaxche, who still fled at the sight of me.

In addition to Spanish, I thought it important that the young should learn Náhuatl, the language of the Aztéca.

This people, whom the nobles and priests feared and spoke of with awe, lived in the mountains far to the west, but sooner or later we would need to deal with them, either as friends or as enemies. The only man among us who spoke Náhuatl was Chalco, the high priest. Like Don Luis, he was reluctant to take on the duties of teaching and taming a roomful of wild young Mayans.

"These offshoots of noble families barely speak their own language," he said. "They speak the words as if they were a mouthful of hot pebbles. How am I to teach them the beautiful words of the Aztéca?"

"Try," I said. "You're a resourceful man. And I hope you can find the time to teach me also. Perhaps one hour in the evening we could talk Náhuatl."

At the close of our first evening together, Chalco brought up the subject of the Tikan prisoners.

"The festival day of Xipe Totec," he said, "is two months away. But I am preparing for it now. How many slaves have you given me?"

"None," I said.

His jaw tightened. "We used up all we had, Lord of the Evening Star, when we celebrated your return. There are none left, except two cripples. We cannot honor the mighty god of spring with creatures that lack arms and legs."

He was wearing the mask of a jungle bird with a long

beak. It had tipped back on his head and he paused to slide it into place.

"Unless the god of spring is generously honored, when the seeds are planted they will not sprout. There will be no harvest and the people will starve."

"How many slaves do you wish?"

"Fifty is a good number."

"I'll give it thought," I said, "and speak to you tomorrow about it."

The two squads of prisoners had accomplished wonders in the short time they had been working. They had stored away the broken columns that littered the great plaza, cleaned the debris from the palace and the Temple of Kukulcán. But there was much more for them to do. I had projects for a thousand more, two thousand. To give up fifty workers was out of the question.

"Ten slaves," I said when we met again the next evening. "No more."

"May I select those I want, the tallest ones? The Tikans tend to be small."

"Select as you wish, but no more than ten."

Chalco was wearing a monkey mask, which, after the bird and jaguar masks he usually wore, gave him an almost human look.

"With ten," he said, "there'll be a poor harvest."

"Ten," I said.

"You could capture more slaves now that you have the big canoe with wings. There are many villages to the north. And there are places inland where you could gather up many, like Palemké and Uxmat."

"Ten," I said.

"Your people will complain when they hear that it is only to be that small number."

"Let them," I said.

These were ill-considered words.

$$\overset{\bullet}{\underset{\rule{2em}{0.4pt}}{\rule{2em}{0.4pt}}}$$

The city greeted my victory with the wildest acclaim.

For a week the populace chanted night and day, the temple drum never ceased to boom. The elders were praiseful. Even the three high priests had praiseful words, though Chalco, lest I think that I had gained a victory over him and the stars, was prompt with an explanation.

"It was the fault of Xelba, my assistant," he said. "Xelba, a dull fellow, committed mistakes and confused the month of Yaax with the month of Quej. In that way a wrong prediction was born."

Suddenly the big drum that shook the bones, the trumpets that pierced the ears, fell silent. Cantú brought word that people had begun to ask questions.

"What was to be done with the Tikan slaves?" they asked. "Why had they not been sacrificed?" "Was Kukulcán saving them for the festival of Xipe Totec?"

It was true that the plaza sparkled. For the first time in centuries the temple was clean. My palace had been saved from ruin. But when, the populace wanted to know, would the many slaves climb the steps to the godhouse and give up their hearts to the hungry sun?

Cantú brought word that they had learned that only ten of the slaves were to be sacrificed in honor of the spring god, Xipe Totec.

Seeds would die in the ground, it was said. There would be no harvest.

To silence the grumbling, I had three crosses made of black, tough-fibered wood, twice my height. One was placed at the harbor, where it could be seen from the strait and by all those who entered or left. The second cross was placed on the terrace, where the priests would have to pass it on their way to and from the godhouse and where the crowds below would see it. The third cross was set above the palace door, so that it caught the sun and cast shadows throughout the day.

A picture of the Virgin Mary, painted by Ceela using a model she found in the palace kitchen, with blue eyes and golden hair and a shimmering halo around her head, was hung from a ceiba tree in the center of the plaza.

I went there at evening for a week and told the people about the Mother of Christ, and who Christ was and how He had died on a cross and why He had died.

My words were much like those I once had spoken to Ceela Yaxche. And like those words, they fell upon ears of stone.

Oh, yes, the plaza overflowed with Indians. They

pressed in upon the guards who were there to protect me from being trampled beneath adoring feet. They listened, not in silence but with murmurs of approval — *ayec, ayec* — and sighs of contentment. They fell to their knees when I fell to mine. They stayed after I had sung the Ave Maria and, striking up their drums, chanted my name.

These services did nothing, however, toward answering the question of the slaves. If anything, the complaints increased. The loudest came from the band of nobles.

In Seville, most of the nobles belonged to a secret society that cared for the poor and the sick and buried the friendless dead. Through the Council of Elders I formed a similar society in the city and thus dampened some of the grumbling.

The farmers were subject to soldierly duties, but had much time on their hands between harvest and planting. Again through the elders, I passed a decree that they should give one day of work each week to the city, to be used as the *bacab,* who took his orders from me, saw fit.

This helped to suppress the complaints but did not end them.

The dwarf suggested that we start a poc-a-tok tournament.

"The season comes later, when the rains settle the dust," he said. "But we could start the games now and thus give the people something else to think about."

I was certain that Cantú's suggestion arose partly from his enthusiasm for the contest, but I also remembered from readings in history that Nero had successfully diverted trouble by furnishing entertainment, circuses, and athletic games for his subjects.

"Where is the game played?" I asked him. "Who plays it? Who watches?"

"The poc-a-tok court is the only edifice in the city that's been completely restored," he said. "It seats a thousand spectators. That is, the nobles and their families sit."

"And the commoners stand?"

"Yes, at both ends of the court. But everyone bets, those who sit and those who stand. The nobles bet houses and jewels and gold. The rabble bets a handful of beans."

The game, as Cantú described it, was played by two teams of heavily padded men, their object being to put a ball through hoops set high in the opposite walls, not using their hands, only hips and shoulders.

"It's a war," Cantú said. "Many are injured and someone is always killed. At the end there's a celebration for the victorious team. The captain is invited to go into the stands and demand from the nobles whatever he sees that he covets. The captain of the defeated team is bound and tied to a post. Then archers range around and shoot arrows at him until he looks like a pincushion."

"It sounds bloodier than the sacrificial altar," I said, and without further comment gave up the idea of the poc-a-tok tournament.

From Ah den Yaxche I learned of a town on the mainland coast some twenty leagues to the north. It was called Zaya and was thought to have a straggling population of two or three hundred.

Forthwith, I summoned the *nacom* and with a shipload of warriors set sail for this nearby port.

It developed that Zaya was not a port at all, but a stone fortress located on the very edge of a cliff, with waves pounding the rocks below and sea spray rising against its gray walls. Since it could not be reached from seaward, we fired one shot and sailed north to a beach, where we landed and doubled back.

The fortress enclosed a small temple and a nest of black-robed priests whose hair was so caked with dried blood that it looked not like hair but more like dark-painted wood. The people, who lived outside the walls on small farms of an acre or less, were gaunt and seemed to be starving.

We gathered them up, three hundred and ten in all, counting women and children, and though they protested, got them aboard the *Santa Margarita* and sailed for home.

Among the gathering were two stonemasons, a quarryman, and a farmer who owned a piece of crystal half the size of his hand that he used to focus the sun upon dried moss or shavings, thus saving the arduous labor of turning a drill-stick until it struck fire.

The masons were put to work in the palace repairing walls and broken columns. The quarryman was given five apprentices who I hoped would learn to cut the beautiful soft yellow stone that hardened on exposure, and with which our jungle abounded.

Unfortunately, the three hundred and ten slaves only increased the clamor for more sacrificial victims. And in the end, after two weeks of haggling with Chalco, I added five more to his list of those who would climb the steps to the godhouse.

Flocks of green parrots flew out of the west at dawn on the morning that the high priests had set as the beginning of spring. A bad omen, they decided, so the festival was delayed for two days, though the heralds of spring were everywhere — in the meadows and the jungle and on the wind, which was sweet with the scent of night-blooming flowers.

The day of Xipe Totec, whose name means The Dear One Slayed, began with the booming of the temple drum and the shriek of trumpets. Before dawn crowds filled the square. They sang and danced and chanted over and over:

> Xipe Totec, god of spring,
> Make ready for thy golden garb.

His statue stood in the middle of the square, at the top of a small stone temple. It was painted in the bright colors of spring, but the face was scarified by deep gashes from jaws to forehead and, as if winded after a long struggle with a powerful foe, the mouth gaped open.

At noon, while the big drum boomed out the hour, Chalco came forth from the temple and down the three steps, followed by a host of attendants, all of them in gowns of the same golden color as ripening maize.

In their midst was one of our most stalwart warriors,

whom I recognized as a man I had once used to carry messages, a handsome and fleet-footed youth, by name Alua.

The young man was naked except that he had a garland of flowers in his hair and a green cypress branch in his hand. Four of the attendants took hold of him and stretched him out on the lower step of the temple. With a sharp knife, high priest Chalco removed his heart and dropped it into a votive cup.

The youth was then dragged up the steps and taken within the temple. As the crowd cheered, clowns and dwarfs and boys on stilts cavorted around the square.

Fifteen men were sacrificed that hour on the temple steps, all of them prisoners I had taken at Tikan and Zaya.

When this was over, the door of the temple opened, a figure appeared, turned to face the four directions, came quickly down the steps — I recognized the snake tattoos on both shoulders as belonging to the warrior Alua — and began to dance, moving his knees stiffly up and down to the tune of flutes.

I was puzzled that this graceful youth should move so awkwardly. Then I saw it was not Alua I was watching, but a smaller man. While Chalco was removing the hearts of the fifteen prisoners, his attendants had delicately flayed the young warrior Alua and draped his skin upon one of the priests.

The priest danced until sunset, moving in wild circles, arms and legs flapping, to the sound of flutes and drumbeats, until he could dance no longer and with a groan collapsed on the stones in a dripping heap.

The following day farmers slashed their fields with stone knives and burned the slashings. Smoke billowed up and hung in a pearly mist above the city. When the fires died out, they punched holes in the earth, dropped in the maize seeds, and tamped them down with their heels.

The god of spring having been honored, their days of labor at an end, they then sat contented in their huts and waited for rain.

It was the first month of the rainy season, but the rains did not come. Clouds, pinnacles and battlements of clouds, rose over the island, hung there every afternoon for days, and mysteriously disappeared.

In this way more than two weeks passed. Then Chalco, the Aztéca, came to me dressed in the gown that he had not changed since the day of the sacrifices.

"Xipe Totec takes revenge upon us," he said. "He lets us know what he thinks of our miserly tribute."

"Fifteen slaves is not a miserly tribute."

Chalco made a hissing sound between his teeth. "Last spring we sacrificed twice that number, and the year before we sacrificed forty-one. The cornstalks were so heavy with ears they bent to the ground."

We haggled for days as the clouds rose up and strangely disappeared.

On all the hundreds of farms that enclosed the city, not a single sprout broke through the hard, dry earth. The farmers watched the skies and waited. Then Cantú brought news that they had begun to sacrifice rabbits and monkeys, even the dogs they kept for food, hoping to placate the angry god of spring.

"Give Xipe Totec a few more hearts," he pleaded. "Perhaps ten or twelve. Then if it doesn't rain they won't blame you."

"They blame me?"

"They have no one else to blame. They can't blame Chalco. They know that he pled with you for more slaves. And they can't very well blame Xipe Totec."

In the end I consented and ten more prisoners were sacrificed, again in the horrible rite of flaying a dead warrior. The farmers were satisfied, the elders and nobles and priests were satisfied.

And yet the drought continued. Xipe Totec was deaf.

Rain clouds drifted out of the east, passed over the island, and disappeared into the west, never pausing. There was enough maize left over from the past to feed the people, but there would be no harvest in the fall and in the spring no seed to plant.

I prayed at night when I went to bed and at dawn when I rose. To no avail. The drought went on and deepened.

In desperation I sent out a call for everyone to come and pray to God, the Lord above all, above Itzamná and Ix Chel and Xipe Totec. Their souls, if they had souls, were steeped in darkness. Whether God would hear them I did not know. He had not heard me. He was as deaf as Xipe Totec. But in His infinite mercy He might hearken to their pleas, though they were not Christians.

They came from all parts of the island and filled the square and the streets and the byways. We prayed, ten thousand people, together on our knees with hands upraised, asking God's mercy.

No one went to the sacrificial stone that day. There were no dancers in bleeding skins. Yet after our prayers, at dusk, lightning streaked across the sky, the heavens parted, and the island rumbled and shook to the sound of thunderous rain.

It was a time to rejoice!

Seeds stirred in the earth and burst their heavy husks. They sent pale shoots into the sunlight.

Likewise, Christ stirred in the dark, pagan souls. Crowds came to the plaza each evening to kneel beside the image of the Virgin. I taught them how to touch their foreheads and their hearts and then their shoulders in the sign of the cross. I sang the Salve Regina in my best voice.

The crowds grew larger day by day. Men and women who had never seen the city before came out of the jungle, carrying children on their backs. They camped in the plaza and their fires shone at night. They pricked their fingers with thorns and held them to the sun at dawn, but in the evening they came to watch and listen.

The maize was waist-high, the ears just forming, when

the rains stopped. Clouds piled up as before and vanished. The maize stalks began to wither. I prayed twice each day for rain, at dawn and dusk, the people gathered around me, but no rain fell.

Foreseeing a scanty harvest, the Council of Elders decided to double the size of our fishing fleet and dry the catch for winter.

When the drought continued, when the crowds that had come to the services thinned out, and the dwarf again brought me rumors of fear and growing discontent among the farmers, I gave up seven of my Tikan workers to the rain god, Chacmool.

A statue of the god stood at the east end of the plaza, facing the direction of the wind that brought rain. He reclined on a bench, resting on his back with his knees drawn up. The seven hearts were placed in his lap, but Chacmool's anger was not appeased.

The drought continued. The season of rain came to an end. It was then that Chalco appeared in the throne room, knelt before me, and set forth a strange idea.

"There is a crop grown in Tenochtitlán," he said. "They call it *tecuítcal*. It grows in one of the three lakes that surround the Aztéca capital. The lake that's salty. It looks like moss and grows very fast."

"It sounds like kelp," I said, wondering what the high priest was up to.

"It's moss, not kelp, and green. It's very nourishing and also tasty if you mix it with chili peppers. The Mexíca eat much of it. In the large salt lagoon north of the harbor we could build dikes to regulate the tides and plant this moss. It grows while you watch. Since the harvest has failed, the city needs something to eat besides smoked fish. I will undertake a journey to Tenochtitlán and bring back a load of this *tecuítcal,* if you wish."

Chalco spoke with such enthusiasm that it set me to thinking.

It was most surely a wild scheme. Had he brought it up as an excuse to make a journey to Tenochtitlán? Had he some secret reason for going? Would he have an audience with Emperor Moctezuma? Was there a scheme with the Emperor to weaken my hold on the island? A scheme with Ah den Yaxche?

I harbored these suspicions for days, but finally sent him off with forty stout porters to bring back forty jugs of *tecuítcal.* The *Santa Margarita* carried him and his porters northwestward for sixty leagues and set them ashore. I was glad to be rid of him and quietly hoped that he might be delayed on the journey. I had little faith in the project.

In his absence I took the opportunity to have two statues torn down and dumped in the lake.

One was a hideous likeness of the flayed Xipe Totec, the other a statue in front of the building that housed the archives, which I could see through the trees from the palace windows. It was carved of red sandstone and showed the god of war on his return from battle, dragging behind him by their hair, with the help of a pair of fanged serpents, a dozen captives who had lost their feet.

While this took place, a *pplom* who had been trading along the mainland shore some forty leagues to the west brought news that in the village of Uxmat heavy rains had fallen during the summer and the maize crop was bountiful.

A once flourishing town, it also had been abandoned and in time, like Zaya and the City of the Seven Serpents, was engulfed by jungle. A scattering of farmers and priests had returned over recent years to live among the ruins and now, according to the trader, numbered more than two hundred.

I ordered the *nacom* to select the best, those with skills other than farming. He sailed off with his warriors, was gone three weeks, and came back from Uxmat with the entire population, some one hundred and fifty Indians, including three priests that we did not need.

Thoughtfully, he brought along the maize that had been harvested, which would help us to feed them and would furnish seed for a spring planting.

He also brought a piece of interesting news he had received from a band of Aztéca traders.

They had met near Uxmat a white man named Gerónimo de Aguilar, who had been cast ashore some time before from the wreck of a caravel. Since he was not a member of the *Santa Margarita*'s crew, it meant that a second Spanish ship had foundered on the coast, not far away and recently.

The news served as a spur to action. When the dwarf heard it, he turned pale.

"I was the first Spaniard to be a castaway," he said. "You were the second. Now we hear of a third. There may be others. In a year's time, in months, hordes of Spaniards will be buzzing around the island like hornets around a honey pot."

95

Cantú was for acting at once.

"Let us take the gold to Cuba," he said. "Have it assayed and registered, the King's fifth duly weighed and stamped and delivered to the Governor of Hispaniola. The rest sent to Spain for safekeeping."

"We risk the ship," I objected, "if we send her off with our Indian crew. They are good seamen in coastal waters, but Cuba is far and hazardous, Spain out of the question."

Instead, I gave immediate attention to the wall that, except for a short distance at the mouth of the harbor, surrounded the city. It was overgrown by jungle but solid, twelve feet high and ten feet in width, with squat towers every quarter of a league arranged to enfilade with sweeping fire an attack from the front or either side.

The people of Uxmat, including the priests, I had the *bacab* put to work hacking trees and creepers from the walls and replacing the stones that had fallen.

I robbed the *Santa Margarita* of four cannon and two falconets and had them placed in a position facing the harbor, whence an attack might be expected, yet easily movable from one tower to another the entire length of the wall, which exceeded one league and a half.

As soon as this task was completed the Uxmat workers joined those from Tikan and Zaya, who were unearthing the buried temple.

At this time, while Chalco was still away, I issued an order through the Council of Elders decreeing that all priests henceforth must spend one day each week in the work force, as I had required of the farmers.

This idea grew out of my readings of Marcus Aurelius, emperor of mighty Rome. "That which doth not hurt the city itself," he wrote, "cannot hurt any of its citizens." And now, forced to make decisions and often doubting that they were wise, I remembered that his son Commodus inherited the crown of the vast Roman Empire when he was only a youth of nineteen.

For a time I went into the jungle and held services for the workers at the temple they were unearthing. But their work was hard and the men were too tired to listen, so I gave this up.

I still appeared in the plaza to greet each dawn and pray to God on my knees. I had Ceela darken the skin of the Virgin, Whose picture hung there, in the thought that by giving Her the dusky look of a Maya, she would have a special attraction for the Indians.

And She did attract them. They came, bringing small gifts, and decked Her brow with jungle blooms. But when the first light shone in the east, they pricked their fingers with thorns and offered their blood to the sun.

Then one morning after I had prayed and sung the Salve Regina and watched my audience raise their bleeding hands to the east, I was struck by a singular thought. I was dismayed that it had not come to me before.

Why, I asked myself, was I there before a pagan crowd, praying on my knees, raising my voice to heaven in their behalf? I was still a student. Never having been ordained, I was not permitted to say mass and conduct rites. In all truth, I was pretending to be a priest, when in fact I was simply a callow seminarian.

It was then that there came to me out of my readings, long ago, in my first year at the seminary, a thought put down by Augustine, Bishop of Hippo.

"God," he said, "judged it better to bring good out of evil than not to permit any evil to exist."

Thus it must be true that evil exists because God has willed it. If this were not true, then there would only be good to choose from, which is no choice at all.

God had created the Maya as He had created all beings. He must have allowed them, therefore, to dwell in darkness, worshipers of a hundred idols, ten times a hundred. In His wisdom, He had given them a choice between good and evil.

Myself, I could point the way, as I had done, between the two kingdoms, one of eternal love, one of the sulfurous pit of pain and despair. But who was I to do more? After all, I was only a seminarian, a neophyte without the mission and the authority of a priest. It was better to stand humbly by and let God's power quietly possess them.

Or so I reasoned in an effort to forget that I had failed to end their bloody rites.

After that, I turned my back on the barbarous rites of sun worship, no longer blaming myself for acts I could not prevent, and spent more time in the palace, studying the books brought to me from the archives.

Most of them had been assembled in the years 1034 to 1146 A.D. These were the years that interested me, since during this period the Maya quit building their beautiful temples and began to abandon their cities one by one.

What had happened to bring this exodus about?

I satisfied myself that they had not met with disasters, such as earthquakes and floods and wars, or with crop failures that led to starvation. Something else had come upon them, and not suddenly.

It was my suspicion that slowly, over a period of a hundred years, the cities had decayed from within. Judging from the hundreds of priests that swarmed through the Temple of Kukulcán clad in filthy gowns that they never changed, the decay might have been caused by a loss of faith.

Furthermore, could the ancient priests have used the stars to make a prediction or a series of predictions — as wrong as the one about the battle of Tikan — that caused the populace to turn against them? When they could no longer trust the priests, did they revolt, withhold their labor, and stop worshipping at the temples? Or, for some strange reason, had they turned against the gods themselves?

It was a great and fascinating mystery. It had a great bearing on the very things I was trying to accomplish.

I was interested in how the city had been governed during its years of splendor. And who governed it? What taxes were collected, and from whom? What work was required of the common man? Did it have alliances with other cities? What was the nature of the goods it bought and sold? What did the city look like before it was engulfed by the jungle?

To my disappointment, I found no answers to these questions.

The scribes who painted the books were only interested in the names of the rulers, the battles they fought, the number of captives they took, their victories — shown by a glyph of a temple with smoke rising — and the stars. The stars that ruled their lives from birth to death.

I set about recording the history of the island from the hour I had appeared, since no records were being kept at the moment, except by the astrologers who nightly read the heavens.

I had difficulties in finding recorders and was forced to settle upon a man who was nearly blind but was acquainted with the Maya glyphs, and on Ceela Yaxche, who did not understand the glyphs but could paint. As she became more skilled in the use of Spanish, I proposed to have the books put down in both Castilian and Maya.

We had difficulty with paper. The early books, those painted four centuries before, were painted on fawnskin, which was as smooth as velvet and pleasing to the eye and touch. Since the art of making it had been lost, we settled for a coarser paper made from the bark of the fig tree.

Events worthy of being painted were gathered by Ah den Yaxche.

I still did not trust the old man. At any moment he could change his mind and decide that for the good of the city it was his duty to expose me. But I finally permitted him to go into the streets and bring back whatever news he could find. He gave me the information, which was usually meager, and I decided what should be painted.

The only news of importance that he brought in during late summer and the month of November came from the constable of the stockade where Don Luis de Arroyo was kept.

Don Luis appeared at the palace punctually every day to teach the class in Spanish, but at night, with the help of two companions, he had used his time to dig a hole through the bottom of his cage and a tunnel that led out of the stockade. The dirt that the three removed, using their hands until their fingers were worn to the bone, they concealed in the depths of the latrine.

On the day when the old man gave me this news I had Don Luis brought to the palace. "Señor," I said, "I understand that you are a good teacher of Spanish."

Arrogant as I had ever seen him, though his elegant clothes were now threadbare and at my request his scabbard was empty, Don Luis smiled.

"Your students like you," I said. "They seem to have learned something of our mother tongue."

He made a slight bow.

"Otherwise," I said, "I would see that your heart is removed. In two weeks, there's a festival to honor the goddess Ix Chel. An excellent time to attend to this matter."

Don Luis smiled again. "A bad time, *amigo*. I still have much to teach the little savages. Their tongues have been twisted out of shape by such words as *Tlancualpican* and *chalchitiuacuecan*. I will need another year, at least, to get them into proper shape."

The temple's huge drum noted the hour of twilight, five resounding booms that shook the walls and the stones of the floor.

"A different sound from the silvery bells of Seville," the young nobleman observed. "Do you ever think of them? Probably not, now that you have the big drum to remind you of the hours."

He began to pace the room, his hand resting on the empty scabbard. Shadows were falling and I could not see his eyes, but they must have shone with a bitter light. He stopped and came close and stood looking down at me.

"I hear," he said, "that you never leave this gloomy place. That you spend your time here poring over the books I see scattered around, and on your knees in prayer. And pray you should! For you deal with creatures that are barely human."

"Creatures who are barely human," I said angrily, "don't build beautiful temples. Nor do they keep track of time — the months and years and centuries — better than we Spaniards do."

Don Luis blinked in mock surprise. "I am pleased to hear you speak as a Spaniard. I was afraid that you had begun to think of yourself as an Indian. I thought you had forgotten that you were born on my farm and studied in a seminary that my great-great-great grandfather built."

Don Luis began to pace again through the cavernous room, a hand on his empty scabbard. He paused at a window and glanced out at the cliff beyond the lake, where a full moon was rising. Emboldened by my silence, he came back and stood over me.

"These barbarians listen," he said, "they dumbly listen while you sing the Ave Maria. Then they go back to their huts and sing the monstrous songs they learned in the cradle. They look at the picture of the Virgin, our Protectress, and titter among themselves because she is not cross-eyed and slant-headed. The crosses you erect here and there are like the Maya cross except that one has bulbous ends and the other hasn't. The Indians see no difference between the two. Ours is the cross of Christ. Theirs is a sign, a marker, to show where two roads come together. And for the Indian, this is what the cross will always mean. Not what, with all your exhortations, you wish it to mean — not the symbol of salvation and life everlasting."

Quietly, hiding my anger, I motioned the guards to take him back to his cage. At the far end of the room he pulled away and turned to face me.

"Do not forget," he said, "through all this masquerade, that you are still a Spaniard and a Christian."

"And do not forget," I said, "that if you dig more holes in your cage, you will likewise dig your grave."

"Your own may not be long delayed," he answered. "There are those who at this moment are quietly preparing it."

"You among them!" I said.

He was taken off, leaving me in an anger that persisted through supper. It changed into a spiritless mood that lasted until one of the servant girls, who had given birth to a boy, brought him forth to show me.

Kneeling, holding up the infant, she said shyly, "You see I have not put his head between the boards. Nor has he a dangling bead to gaze at."

"Why is this?" I said.

"Because," she said, "I want him to look like the Lord of the Evening Star."

There was nothing I had done, the prayers I had prayed and the crosses I had erected, that meant so much to me as these words spoken by the kitchen maid.

I did not let this happening blind me to the angry threat that Don Luis had shouted as he left the chamber that morning. Chalco was surely behind the plotting, but there were others among his assistants who might also wish me dead.

The dwarf treated the threat more seriously than I did. He took it upon himself to appoint a food taster to sit at table and sample all the food that came in. Although this protected me from violent poisons that acted immediately, it did nothing about the poisons that required weeks, even months, to work their way.

"There are no such poisons on our island," the dwarf assured me when I reminded him of this fact. "We have neither mercury nor arsenic. Everything is sudden here, like the poisons the Indians use to tip their arrows. It kills a monkey within seconds, a man in minutes."

I soon grew tired of the food taster — a toothless old man who wore earrings that rattled as he moved his jaws, who made munching sounds when he tasted, and smacked his fat lips when he finished. Tired of waiting for him either to be seized by deathly spasms or to go on eating.

After he was dismissed I forgot about the warning Don Luis had shouted at me. Then unexpectedly on a bright morning while larks were singing in the flame trees just outside the window, as I was about to use the movable toilet that one of the servants had brought in, I was forcefully reminded of it. Looking down I saw below me the glint of two shining eyes, the flick of an orange-tinted tongue. It was a water snake, not much longer than the length of my middle finger, but a deadly snake, the one the Indians called Seven Curses.

The servant was dragged in and queried, but he knew nothing about the snake. He had received the cabinet from a servant, who had received it from a servant, who had taken it from someone else, and so on. We never found the culprit.

I took precautions against this bizarre incident happening again, but quickly forgot that my life was in danger. My spirits were enlivened by a second woman who came to show me that she no longer put her child's head between boards or dangled beads before his eyes.

Someday I would rule over a citizenry that was no longer slant-headed and cross-eyed. I had made a small start on that long road.

I had more than a start, however, on the first of my excavations. The workmen brought from Tikan, Uxmat, and Zaya, numbering nearly two thousand, had already cleared a road leading from the plaza through a jungle of thorn bushes and creepers to the outskirts of the buried temple.

A stand of cypress trees had sprouted from its roof, with a nest of spiny agave clustered around their trunks. These had been cut away and burned. Columns that had fallen over the centuries and lay hidden under mounds of moldering leaves had been dug up and put aside to use again. A wide staircase, the main one of three that led into the temple, stood revealed, glistening white as the day the *antiguos* who built it put down their hammers.

To my great surprise, however, what was thought to be a temple turned out to be not a temple but a mammoth observatory. Because it was built with a rounded, shell-like dome, it reminded me of a snail. I therefore named it El Caracol, and thus Ceela put it down in the book of excavations she had begun for the year of our Lord 1519, in the reign of Kukulcán, God of the Evening Star.

El Caracol rested on a platform twice my height, which in turn sat upon one somewhat shorter. The whole edifice measured a hundred and six paces in length and half that number in width. It was made of fitted stone, ochre in cast, and still retained some of its original color — a light sea-green — and around the doorway, yellow bands in the shape of sleeping serpents.

A winding ramp led upward to a circular room, pierced by four apertures facing the cardinal points of the compass — north, south, east, and west. It was through these slits in the stone that the priests had watched the stars and made their observations.

At the foot of the ramp a passage led down to a wide landing, to a second landing, and a third. Here, when the dwarf and I were inspecting El Caracol for the first time, we were confronted by a pair of alligators larger than life, carved from sandstone and fitted with green jade teeth, crouching on either side of a massive door, their open jaws enclosing a human head.

The door had double panels and in the center of one was the print of a bright red hand.

Half the size of mine, with the fingers spread out so as to show the clear lines of the palm, it was, according to Cantú, the mark, the signature of the architect who had built the observatory. I was to find this red hand in all the buildings we excavated, sometimes in a prominent place for everyone to see, often hidden away in a corner.

The door, which was jammed by fallen stones, was broken open, and we entered a vaulted room that extended far beyond the reach of our torches. In the center of this vast room I made out what seemed to be a small godhouse.

"A tomb," the dwarf shouted, his words flying off into the darkness and returning in a ghostly echo. "A king's tomb!"

That is what he saw in the dim light and what he wanted to see — the sarcophagus of a mighty king, filled with treasure.

But it was neither a godhouse nor a king's sarcophagus. It was a ship, more than twenty paces in length, with a high bow and stern, woven of reeds arranged in bundles heavily tied and set down in pitch.

On a raised deck in the center of this canoelike ship,

with his back against a broken mast, sat a figure dressed in white. A plumed cap draped the skull and a tuft of dusty hair jutted forth from the jaws. In his lap, he held a delicate fan.

I gasped. For a moment I saw Ah den Yaxche sitting there in a regal gown, his white beard curled, a replica of the drawing I had seen of an Egyptian prince. But the embroidered gown clothed a skeleton, and the beard adorned a gaping jaw.

We did not remain long. The dry air burned our skins. The smoke from our torches and the dust we raised choked us.

When we went again to the tomb it was to decipher a glyph on the prow of the ship. The day of the entombment was carved in Maya. It gave, counting in our time, the year 211 after the birth of Christ.

The ship was wholly unlike the Maya dugouts in size, construction, and materials. The bearded figure in the long white robe, embroidered with signs I had never seen before, did not look like a Maya. If he was not a Maya, who could he be? An Egyptian? If so, why was he here in the heart of an ancient city?

Cantú clamored to search the tomb for gold and jewels, but to his great distress I decided to seal the door for the present.

Ceela entered the discovery of the ship in our archives and left room for any answers to these questions that time and study might develop.

The Indians were promptly put to work on the excavation of another mound, much larger than the observatory, which lay a short distance to the west and was connected to it by a raised causeway.

There was a line of mounds beyond this one. Between the Temple of Kukulcán and the palace was the mound with the red roof and others that the dwarf had shown me the day I arrived. Dozens of mounds were visible from the temple godhouse, stretching away into the jungle in all directions.

But I needed workmen to unearth them, at least three times the number that I now had. I inquired among our *pochtéca,* who were trading along the coast, if they knew of any villages where prisoners could be taken.

There was none large enough to bother with, they said, but they suggested that I consider an attack upon the city of Mayapán, which lay inland and some one hundred and ten leagues to the northwest.

For many centuries in the past, I was told, Mayapán had been the capital of a confederacy of villages, towns, and city-states. But some sixty years ago a chieftain, Ah Xupan, had raised a revolt, claiming that the rulers were not natural lords and that they were selling their own people as slaves to the Aztéca in Tenochtitlán.

As a result, various factions fought bitterly among themselves. The city of Mayapán, which was protected by a twelve-foot wall extending for six Roman miles, had been destroyed from within, the confederacy broken up and now no longer extant. Its former inhabitants were scatterd about, ready, so my informants told me, to be rounded up and taken prisoner, one by one.

However, there were several difficulties connected with such a campaign.

The villages of Uxmat and Zaya had been easy to

capture because they were located on the sea, where they could be overpowered by the ship's cannon. Tikan fell to us because its people had learned that a god had appeared among them.

Mayapán presented a different problem.

It was located far from the coast, in mountainous country difficult to reach because of poor trails and a desert of thorn bushes that had to be crossed. Furthermore, though he had not traded there for more than three years, one of my informants was certain that the city had not heard of Kukulcán's return. Otherwise, he said, its people would have made the long pilgrimage to worship at my feet.

I gave up the idea of attacking Mayapán. But the trader's suggestion sparked a line of thought.

Moctezuma had built an empire by conquering provinces beyond the borders of his capital, Tenochtitlán. He ruled dozens of villages, towns, and city-states. As the god Kukulcán, with a more powerful presence than Moctezuma's own, possibly I could restore the confederacy of Mayapán and join it as a vassal to the Island of the Seven Serpents.

Soon afterwards Chalco, the high priest, returned from his native province, a vassal city of Emperor Moctezuma. He brought with him many jugs of *tecuítcal,* borne on the broad shoulders of ninety porters, fifty of them, to my amazement, Aztéca.

Our workmen built an earthen dike across the mouth of the lagoon in the cove north of the city and set out the green, mosslike *tecuítcal* in its brackish water. But when the planting was done and the *Santa Margarita* was ready to take the visitors on the first leg of the journey back to their home, they decided, since it was very cold in the mountains where they lived, that they wished to stay until the end of our beautiful spring.

I made them welcome and put them to work — all were strong young warriors — on the excavation of the second mound.

It was at this time that I decided to make a journey to the Aztéca capital.

The idea of restoring the confederacy of Mayapán and joining it as a vassal to the Island of the Seven Serpents had taken a strong hold upon me. If I could see the great city of Tenochtitlán, if I could talk to its nobles, perhaps to Emperor Moctezuma himself, I would learn by what strategies it had conquered its vassal states and kept them in subjection.

Equally important, I would learn how my own city should be organized.

It ran somewhat better than when I arrived, yet it still was a casual operation. Public servants, for instance — those who gathered copal to burn in the temple, the street cleaners, the drawers of community water — all took long siestas in the middle of the day. Treasury clerks, it was said, made a practice of nibbling small bites out of the city funds. Even Xicalanco, my irreplaceable archivist, filched pieces of our best paper. How, I wondered, did Emperor Moctezuma treat laziness and theft?

Cantú and Ah den Yaxche were strongly opposed to my journey.

"It's a long one, a hundred and fifty leagues or more,"

the dwarf said, "through hot lands where disease is rife and mountains where the snows never melt. Where everyone you meet is a savage. And when you get there, *if* you do get there alive, what happens then with an emperor who slays twenty thousand people in a single day?"

Ah den Yaxche added, "The Aztéca are a warrior race. They have grown powerful by the sword. They live by the sword. The Maya, on the other hand, are .not warriors. Once they were a brilliant people, superior to the Aztéca in every way. But they have lost that brilliance. They are shiftless. They are content to live from one moment to the next. Be satisfied, therefore, to do what can be done with the poor material you have to work with. Do not try to rival the mighty Moctezuma."

Preparation for the journey took less than a week. I first convinced Chalco that it was necessary for me to go to Tenochtitlán, giving the reasons I have just stated.

He was silent for a moment, scarcely believing, I am sure, what he had heard."It's a dangerous journey," he said, repeating the dwarf's words.

"All journeys worth making are dangerous."

Chalco shook his head. I could not see his face, hidden as it was behind his jaguar mask, but I knew that he was overcome by the happy prospect of being rid of me, if only for a time.

"I forget, Knight of the Evening Star, that you are not mortal like the rest of us," he said. "There are no dangers for a god. You should have a safe journey and learn many things from Lord Moctezuma, likewise from Xocoyotl, Cem-Anahuac, Uey-Tlatoani, and the other nobles."

His bearing changed when I told him that he himself must accompany me to Tenochtitlán. "You're an Azte-catl," I said. "You have made the journey. You know Moctezuma. The — "

"I'll send Tlacho to guide you," he broke in. "He's an Aztecatl and knows the best way to Tenochtitlán."

"It is you who will be my guide," I said, speaking not unkindly, even softly, in the words of Náhuatl, his native tongue. "We will leave as soon as possible."

There was no further argument. Chalco bowed grace-fully, made the gesture of kissing the earth at my feet, touched the beak of his jaguar mask.

"We can go now," he said without the least trace of anger, in a servile voice. "Do you wish to go by litter or on the back of the black beast?"

"On foot," I said, "and as a trader."

"That is wise. As the god Kukulcán, you would never reach Tenochtitlán. Thousands would swarm about you. Soon you could not move for people. You would be trampled to death under loving feet. Even worse, every lord, every cacique, of every town and village you passed through would suddenly cease to rule. You would be the supreme god of all. There would be great confusion, battles, death."

I thought it best not to divulge my plans to the popu-lace, dreading the thought of their tears and lamenta-tions.

I warned the Council of Elders to beware of ships that

113

might appear in my absence, to greet all strangers politely, supply them with any food they might need, exchange presents, but under no circumstances to let them set foot in the city.

I asked Ah den Yaxche to tell his granddaughter that she had my permission to ride the stallion while I was away. I also requested him to keep an eye on Don Luis and the fifty Aztéca, of whom I was suspicious, to see that they and the rest of the prisoners kept diligently at work.

We left the harbor at noon and reached the mainland before nightfall, anchoring in a cove protected from a heavy wind. The same crew that I had on the campaign against Tikan sailed with us. The wind held us back as we sailed north along the coast of Yucatán, so we did not turn west until three days later.

We were headed for Ixtlilzochitl, a trading center that Chalco had passed through with his Aztéca porters. We carried as presents for Moctezuma a bag of pearls of the finest orient, jewels that the Emperor was reported to covet.

On a morning of intense heat, the air filled with insects, we entered a winding estuary where the water was a clear blue, showing a sandy bottom at a depth of two fathoms. The trading village lay at the head of the estuary. Here we dropped anchor and furled our sails.

I turned the ship over to the *nacom,* Flint Knife, with the same instructions I had given to the three elders about any white men he might encounter. To keep the hold clean, the sails dry, to wash down the decks every day.

The dwarf begged to stay aboard until I returned, but since he was a man of some sagacity I wanted him with me.

Two days later we were ready to leave but were delayed by a week of torrential rain.

At last, on a clear day of terrible heat, we took the trail for the land of the Aztéca, ten porters carrying our supplies. The pearls, because of their value, were strapped to our waists. We carried black staves, the insignia of the merchant trade, although we had nothing to trade.

I had left my mask on the *Santa Margarita,* but Chalco wore his until we had slogged through a sickly yellow marsh infested with water snakes and the village lay well behind us.

What I expected to see hidden behind his jaguar mask, I do not know. I had never formed any idea of what he looked like, nor had I tried. Possibly a nose like the head of a stone club, a slanting forehead. Surely, the small and predatory eyes of a jungle cat lurked there.

He wrapped his mask in plantain leaves and set about stowing it away in one of the packs. When he had finished, he turned and said something.

In my amazement, I failed to hear.

Before me stood a man much younger than I had thought, whose face was neither tattooed nor scarified as I had expected. It was the face of an artisan, a goldsmith or a painter of books or of one who could carve the delicate golden hummingbirds that many of our nobles wore around their necks.

Yes, the mask had hidden the sensitive face of an artisan. Without it Chalco was a different person, no longer the haughty and mysterious high priest.

He smiled a modest, almost bashful smile that I am compelled to say seemed engaging. Small wonder that he wore a mask with catlike eyes and terrifying fangs.

We left the hot salt marshes and were traveling fast when we came upon a herd of young deer. We had plentiful supplies of maize cakes and dried fish, but Chalco insisted upon killing two of the animals. It was not this that held us up, but the ritual afterwards.

The porters laid the deer out in the grass, straightened their crumpled legs, and placed maguey leaves around the bodies in the four directions. It was an apology for the act of killing, made to the animals who were dead in the name of the living, honoring the law which decreed that all life was sacred, kin one to the other — the leaves of the maguey, the deer, ourselves.

"We are cousins of the deer," Chalco said, "and drink the same water that they drink."

Coming from a man who had argued that it was better to sacrifice a hundred prisoners than fifty, these words surprised and puzzled me.

We traveled out of the low country in good order now that the salt marshes lay behind us.

In two days we covered more than twelve leagues, but this pace proved too fast for the dwarf's short legs and we had to rest for a day in the village of Socochima. I myself was glad to rest, for after months of a soft life in the palace, doing little more strenuous than lifting books and walking from one room to the other, I was ill conditioned.

In addition to blistered feet and aching muscles, I was discomfited by crowds of curious villagers, who were not content until they had viewed me from all sides, loudly commented on my height, white skin, and long blond hair, and finally touched my garments or my bare skin.

I was further annoyed.

I had become used to people approaching me with downcast eyes, bowing in a gesture of kissing the earth, and backing away when they were dismissed. I was somewhat surprised at myself for feeling this way, but it did not lessen my annoyance at the lack of reverence these people showed.

Beyond the village of Socochima we began to climb and in five days entered a pass through high mountains. There it rained and then hailed, and a bitter wind blew from the heights.

We changed into warmer clothes, which Chalco had wisely brought along, and thus kept from freezing. The dwarf complained bitterly at the cold and sulked, groaning that he wished to return to the ship. I had a notion to send him back, but fortunately thought better of it.

At the end of the pass we came to Xocotlán and were now in the heart of the Aztéca, Chalco informed us.

The lord of the province was Ozintec, a young man with red-tinted hair hanging to his waist. He greeted Chalco warmly, apparently having known him before, but his gaze quickly fastened upon me.

"What price do you wish for the giant?" he asked Chalco.

"He is not for sale," Chalco said.

"You will sell him to the Emperor, though."

"He is not for sale."

"The dwarf?"

"Equally, Lord Ozintec."

The dwarf said in Spanish, "I think the *bastardo* would like to sell us."

"It's possible."

"Let's strangle him," the dwarf said. "I will do it tonight when he sleeps. Then we'll return to the *Santa Margarita* and engage in no more tramping for a year or so."

Socochima had two small temples on a plaza facing

each other. Beside them were piles of human skulls, arranged neatly in rows. I made a guess, as we left the plaza, that there were more than ten thousand of these whitened skulls stacked in the sun.

The next day we made better time, having left the mountains for good and finding ourselves on a plateau. Two snow-crested peaks rose up on the far horizon. We were on our way to the city of Texcála, Chalco said.

"The city is a vassal of Moctezuma, but not a friend. The people hate him and strive for his downfall."

The journey to Texcála was uneventful, and we saw no one except Aztéca runners, who passed us on their way to Tenochtitlán, carrying parcels of fish for the Emperor's table.

We had encountered the runners many times since leaving the coast. They ran in relays, two men in a team, three leagues at a stretch, passing their parcels from one team to another. They made the long journey in two short days.

"We'll at least have fresh-caught fish when we sit down at Moctezuma's table," the dwarf said, trying to make a joke. "If we ever manage to see him, which I doubt."

That night before we reached Texcála, while we were sitting around our campfire, I asked Chalco how he planned to introduce me to the Emperor.

"I have been traveling as a common trader, but I shouldn't be a trader when I meet and talk to Moctezuma."

Chalco took a moment to think. "Not in the guise of a *pochtéca,* no, but I can't introduce you as the god Ku-

119

kulcán. I would not be believed. The Emperor would think me a wild man and forthwith put me in a cage. And you as well."

"He must have heard of me," I said.

"If he has, it is with disbelief."

"Why?" the dwarf shouted angrily. "He *is* a god. He was welcomed into the City of the Seven Serpents as a god."

"Because of you," Chalco said. "You prepared the way. The priests saw momentous things in the stars. People were tired of the quarreling elders. They prayed for the return of the god and were ready to receive him. The Aztéca are not. They are flushed with their own importance. They rule all that they see, even the lands they do not see. They call themselves 'We of the One and Only World' and they believe this fanciful idea."

"How then is he to be introduced?" the dwarf wanted to know.

"He will be an important lord from a far-off Maya province come to pay tribute."

I had not been pleased with my first change of fortune — from a god to a trader — and was not pleased now to be merely a lord of a remote country. Yet I saw the sense of his words and did not bring up the subject again, though the dwarf never ceased to bedevil Chalco about it.

In the morning we started through the vast country of Texcála. A good trail led us past two towering volcanoes, both snow-crested, one of them giving off smoke.

We arrived at a village on the outskirts of Tenochtitlán after three days of hard travel. Here we rested for a day, bathed in a hot spring, changed our travel-worn clothes, and made up for the meals we had not eaten since the last of the deer.

On the next morning, in the bright sunshine, we started down a raised causeway toward Tenochtitlán.

The city shimmered white in the distance, a brilliant white since it rose up from a vast green lake and a myriad of winding canals. Canals ran along either side of the causeway and from time to time we crossed them on wooden bridges.

The dwarf paused in amazement.

"I have seen the great places in many parts of this world," he said, "in Egypt and the cities of Venice, Constantinople, and Rome, but never have I seen a city of such magnificence."

The causeway swarmed with people going into the city on foot. There were so many traveling that little attention was paid to the dwarf or to me, which was a boon to us both.

We reached a second broad causeway, this one at right angles to the road we were on, and here we saw hundreds of canoes, laden with produce, on their way to the marketplace. People walking along the causeway were talking to friends in the passing canoes.

Not far beyond this crossing, where two temples stood opposite each other, we entered a narrow street and at once stepped out into an enormous square. Later, during my days in Tenochtitlán, I paced off its four sides and found that they came to a total of more than three thousand feet. This plaza was enclosed by solid ranks of buildings, richly decorated with sculpture and bas-reliefs of all descriptions.

In the very center of this enclosure stood a pyramid, taller than the Temple of Kukulcán, with crenelated walls of many shades of red, blue, and yellow, with stairs on all four sides that faced the four directions of the world and led upward to a pair of small temples.

The dwarf and I were left in front of this pyramid, beside a pool where silver-sided fish were swimming about. Promising to return shortly, Chalco disappeared with the ten porters at his heels and all but three of our pearls in his possession.

We soon attracted a crowd bemused by my height and the dwarf's shortness. A girl of five or six, black-eyed and brown-skinned, came up and handed me a flower. In return I gave her one of the pearls I had withheld from Chalco.

There were flowers everywhere — growing beside the pool, in baskets strung along the front of the temple, in the doorways of the buildings that enclosed the great square. Among the hundreds who passed, many men carried a bunch of flowers and all the women had flowers in their hair. As we came along the causeway I had seen dozens of canoes filled with roses.

I could not remember ever having seen a flower in the City of the Seven Serpents, except in the hair of the slain young man, an Aztecatl. Certainly the men did not carry them, nor did the women.

When I returned to the island, I would see that not one building or temple was without flowers. The nobles who lived in the palaces and the peasants in their huts would plant them. The priests would learn to tend them. Our soil was rich, the sun strong.

Ya! We would have gardens throughout the city. They would rival, they would surpass, the gardens in Tenochtitlán, I said to myself.

Yet as I gazed out over the swarms of white-clad Indians at the offices and sanctuaries that surrounded the great square, my spirits sank. Ornately carved and beautifully painted, rising side by side in splendid, unbroken rows, these buildings stood in sharp contrast to the square that faced the Temple of Kukulcán, the disorderly jumble of broken pillars and crumbling walls so recently snatched from the jungle.

"To rebuild our city," I said to the dwarf, "will take years. Many years. Unless we can double and triple the number of workers."

The dwarf did not answer. His gaze was fixed upon a passing litter in which a young lord lay stretched out, while servants fanned him with feathered whisks. He wore a gold nose plug, gold rings on his fingers, even his thumbs. From his ears dangled loops of gold, and his hair, knotted on top of his head, was bound with gold pins that glittered as he bounced along.

The dwarf glanced at me. His face shone with the first light I had seen there in days.

"He, he," he said and grinned at some thought of his own.

The morning passed, a cold sun moved overhead, still Chalco did not return.

The dwarf was hungry, not having eaten a bite since breakfast. Vendors strolled everywhere through the crowds selling maize cakes and pink frijoles, but I had nothing to buy them with except a valuable pearl. To stay his hunger he drank from a fountain we found in front of the temple, the water pouring ice-cold from the mouth of a stone goddess.

When Chalco did return, his tunic showing signs of a hearty meal, his face was flushed with excitement.

"Fortune smiles on us," he said, as if he could scarcely believe the news he carried. "This is the day, the one day in the entire month, when the Emperor hears petitions. Not for another month does he meet with visitors from the various parts of his empire. But I have managed to convince Lord Tlaloc, a cousin of the Emperor who is in charge of these matters, that you cannot wait for a month. Important affairs in your country require your lordly attention."

Without further words, he herded us across the square to a door guarded by four stone serpents.

"Speak to the Emperor in Náhuatl," he instructed me. "You speak it hesitantly, but well enough to be understood."

Two lords in feathered regalia met us and led the way along a winding passage, across a bridge that spanned a stretch of black water and a wharf where scows were anchored, into an alcove lit by rows of votive torches.

"You are to make a low bow," Chalco went on. "Touch the palms of your hands on the floor, then raise them and touch your forehead. Do this three times."

"And you," he said to the dwarf, "remain hidden until you are called. Whereupon step forward and present this gift."

Chalco handed him the bag of pearls. "Say that the pearls are a gift from Lord Zamabac. If you forget the name, as you are apt to do, say any name that comes to mind, like Tlacolhtecuhtli, for instance. If you can't think of a name, say nothing and bow yourself out of sight, remembering never to show your back to the Emperor."

"Lord of the Morning," Chalco said, turning to me, "address the Emperor as Great Speaker or Revered Speaker of the One World, for these are titles he likes and is known by. Also you might take notice of his beard. It is an unusual occurrence among the Aztéca for men to be so endowed. Moctezuma's is luxuriant, but he keeps it neatly trimmed and it's as dark as a starless sky. He is very proud of it. You might say, 'Great Speaker,

125

Lord of the Beard.' This will create a favorable impression."

Cantú cleared his throat. "When I was a student in Salamanca, it was said that if a beard were a sign of intelligence, then a goat would be wiser than our great King Carlos."

Cantú laughed, but he was uncomfortable. No more, however, than I.

The alcove was gray with smoke and reeked of incense. I could hear voices on the far side of the door, earnest voices speaking in the strange language of the Mexíca, so like and so unlike the language of the Maya.

"Oh, yes," said Chalco, "as a sign of respect to the Emperor, remove your sandals. It is also customary to appear before him poorly dressed, but you are already in a very ragged state."

The two nobles knocked on the door with gold canes. It swung open at once. Both of them slipped through and the door closed behind them.

After a long wait, during which I heard solemn voices and the reedy wail of flutes, the door opened upon a vista that for a moment blinded me.

The dwarf, standing at my side, said in a choked whisper, "Mary on the Mount, I do not believe what I see."

The room seemed made of gold — the ceiling, the walls, the floor, the air itself — and it all shimmered in the glow of votive urns. Light came from all directions in dazzling streamers. I moved through waves of golden air down a corridor of burning incense, toward a throne where hundreds of golden streamers came together and rested upon a figure in a jaguar robe, a small man with a curly black beard.

The dwarf whispered, "He, he, it is not the palace of Kukulcán we are in!"

Speechless, clad in bedraggled clothes, and bare of foot, I bowed my head. A few steps from the throne, ill at ease, I touched my forehead to the floor, once, twice, three times, the third time with a feeling of humiliation.

From the nobles came gasps of astonishment. And little wonder! When had they seen a young man of my great height, made to look still taller by the dwarf — a man with blue eyes, fair skin, and long blond hair?

Only the Emperor was silent.

Forgetting myself, I glanced at him, then quickly lowered my eyes. But in that brief moment I saw that he was a man of some thirty years, slender yet of a vigorous build. His hair, cut short above his ears, which were pierced by turquoise plugs, was tied in a knot on top of his head. He had a long, copper-colored face and a well-trimmed beard.

"Say something," the dwarf hissed, "lest they think you a dunce."

"Great Speaker, Lord of the Black Beard," I said, using the words that Chalco had given me, "I have traveled far, from a land to the south. I have come to see with my own eyes the Emperor whose name is known to all the world and to ask for his friendship. In token of mine, I offer you this gift from the seas of my country."

The dwarf danced forward with the bag of pearls and handed it to the Emperor.

"I am told," Moctezuma said, "that you are a Maya lord."

"That is true," I answered.

"I have never seen a Maya before. I have heard that they are a sickly breed, but you belie this. Are all the Maya of your height and breadth and of the same hue?"

"Not all."

"I am told that in your country you are a famous warrior."

"A warrior," I lied, modestly.

"You have met many of the enemy?"

"Yes, Revered Speaker."

"How many of the foe have you slain?"

"Twelve," I said, drawing a figure from the air.

"How many have you taken prisoner?"

I counted in my mind, taking my time about it.

"Ciento cinco," the dwarf whispered.

"One hundred and five," I said.

Moctezuma showed no surprise at this incredible number. "Your prisoners were sacrificed to honor Uitzilopochtli?"

I assumed that Uitzilopochtli was the all-powerful Aztéca god. "Yes, Revered Speaker, to give him strength for his journey through the sky."

The Emperor began to tap the toe of his jeweled boot. It glittered in the torchlight and made an ominous sound, the only sound in the quiet room.

"Among the Maya," he said, "is it an honor to die upon the stone? Does the slain warrior become a companion of the eagle? Each day does this soldier fill his hours with song and with mock battles? In time does he

128

become a fleet-winged hummingbird, hovering from bloom to bloom in the summer air?"

The Aztéca world, as Moctezuma described it, was not far different from the world of the Maya. No doubt it was borrowed from us, since as a nation we were thousands of years older.

Still tapping his boot, the Emperor waited for an answer. He had left me no choice, unless I wished to insult him by declaring his bloody rite and its heavenly aftermath a lot of nonsense.

"Cuidado, señor," the dwarf whispered.

I took his advice, saying in a firm voice, "Mighty Lord of the Black Beard, this I believe."

"Do you believe that there is no hatred between the captor and the one who is captured? That when a man takes a prisoner he says to him, 'You are my well-loved son'? And in reply the captive says, 'You are my reverenced father'?"

"Yes," I said, but not believing it.

"Do you believe, young man of the light hair and blue eyes, that a warrior who takes a prisoner and watches him die upon the altar should know that sooner or later he will follow him into the hereafter by the same kind of death? That he should say to this man, 'Today it is you, tomorrow it is me'?"

"Yes, Revered Speaker."

"A lord of Texcála, whose name I have forgotten," the Emperor said, "was taken captive by the Aztéca, but they loved him so much that instead of ending his life they gave him command of an army. However, after his triumphant return from battle, having gained a glorious victory, he would not accept their acclaim. He insisted upon death and died upon the sacrificial stone. Would you, traveler from the country of the Maya, give the same answer?"

I glanced at the Emperor, compelled to do so. Our eyes met for an instant, until with a faint movement of his lips — it was not a smile — he turned away.

An intricately woven gold screen was placed between us. It shut the Emperor off from view and served to end our meeting.

Remembering Chalco's admonition, we backed out of the throne room, making the gesture of kissing the stones as we went.

We were met in the alcove by two guards, who escorted us to a building on the opposite side of the square and showed us to our quarters, which consisted of five rooms furnished with benches, a sheaf of ten wool spreads that could either be slept upon or under, depending upon the weather, and three large rooms where gold urns were burning incense.

"What do you make of our meeting?" the dwarf asked.

"The meeting puzzles me," I said.

It was the first we had spoken since we had left the palace.

"Moctezuma never asked what you did," the dwarf said. "Only if you were a warrior. How do you suppose Chalco introduced us when he arranged the meeting? My guess is he told Moctezuma that we were a pair of freaks — a giant and a dwarf. Did you note how the nobles stared?"

130

"I heard their chatter. One said that I must be an albino and that you, señor, were the handsomest dwarf he had ever seen, not wizened like the others in the royal court. You'll probably end up there," I said, trying to make light of it.

"More likely in the Emperor's zoo."

"Yes, both of us may find ourselves in a cage. I've heard that Moctezuma has thousands of oddities, collected from all over his empire. A man with two heads, a dog with six legs and no tail. We'll make fine additions."

"He, he, he," Cantú said.

I went to a window that looked out upon the square. One bright star showed in the east. A lamplighter was hurrying along with his torch. He passed close and in its glow I saw that the two guards who had shown us to our quarters were standing not far from our doorway.

"We are watched," I said.

The dwarf came to the window and glanced out. The two men had moved away from the light, but their shadows and the shadows of the long obsidian clubs they carried were cast on a nearby wall.

"Do you remember," the dwarf said, "that Moctezuma was only interested in whether you're a warrior or not?"

"I remember."

"And what you thought about a warrior's death? If you were pleased by the thought of being a hummingbird and flying around among the flowers of an eternal spring?"

"I remember, word for word."

It had grown dark in the room. I could not see Cantú's

face, but his voice was suddenly strained.

"I think that the Emperor has plans to offer our hearts to the war god," he said. "We should disappoint him. We should leave and lose no time about it."

I pondered the idea, but before I could answer him, a messenger appeared at the door with news from high priest Chalco. He had gone to the distinguished city of his birth on important business. He would return for us in three days, sufficient time, he hoped, for me to gain some knowledge of Tenochtitlán. Also, he had arranged for one of the nobles to be my escort.

"I think more than ever," the dwarf said, "that we should leave Tenochtitlán without delay."

"Soon, Don Guillermo, when I have learned what I have come here to learn."

At midmorning of the next day, the noble escort Chalco had promised me arrived at our door and introduced himself as Lord Tzapotlan, a nephew of the Revered Speaker, Moctezuma.

In the company of attendants carrying umbrellas — gray skies promised rain — a phalanx of palace attendants with spears, and a pretty girl clutching a basket of flowers, handfuls of which she gave to both Cantú and me, we set forth for the temple of the war god, Uitzilo-pochtli.

The two guards who had slept all night outside our window followed us at a distance.

An army of cleaners were washing off the temple stairs. An army of painters moved along behind them, coating everything with lime and mica that glittered even on this sunless day.

We climbed to the summit of the pyramid — a long, steep climb, some twenty steps higher than the Temple of Kukulcán.

Two small godhouses faced each other and between them stood the sacrificial stone, which the cleaners had not yet washed. The stone and the two broad gutters that led from it to the stairs, thence down the face of the pyramid, were thick with blood from the latest cere-mony. A cluster of priests whose hair and gowns were also caked with blood stared at us from the doorway of one of the godhouses.

God judged it better to bring good out of evil than not to let any evil exist.

"I have heard," the dwarf said to the young lord, "that the Emperor has sacrificed as many as twenty thousand prisoners in a single day."

Lord Tzapotlan laughed. "Twenty thousand in a year, perhaps. In a day the most he ever sacrificed was two thousand. That was when he celebrated the victory over Quaunáhuac."

"I noticed as we came here that painters were at

work," the dwarf said. "You must be making ready to celebrate something important."

"Of special importance," Lord Tzapotlan said. "It's the ceremony held every nineteen days in honor of the war god."

Cantú glanced at me, a wordless message that I did not miss.

"I am sorry that we'll not be here for the ceremony," I said.

For a moment a half-smile played around the mouth of Lord Tzapotlan, but he said nothing in reply. He made a sweeping gesture and said haughtily, "Tenochtitlán!"

And there it was in all its grandeur!

The clouds had burned away. Below me stretched the city, its three encircling lakes and ring of vassal cities.

"It reminds me of Venice, pearl of the Adriatic," said the dwarf, who had visited everywhere in the world, or so he boasted. "It's like something you might see in a dream."

And it *was* a city from a dream — shimmering in the sun, floating on the green waters like a beautiful white flower.

Overcome with unchristian envy, I thought, "And how different from our ruined city!"

Lord Tzapotlan led us down into the pyramid to show me the Emperor's storehouse of skulls, which was many times the size of the one at home. I saw rooms filled with strange gifts from vassal cities, nooks where fanged gods looked out at us, dank corridors lit by votive urns tended by dozens of black-robed priests who flitted about on secret missions, barefooted and reeking like carrion birds.

The second day was of more interest. We visited the marketplace with its hundreds of stalls and mountains of produce, much of it grown on the small islands that dotted the lakes. Of special interest to me were enormous mounds of a watery substance that looked like green scum. This was *tecuítcal,* the plant that Chalco had brought from the city and planted in our lagoon.

The armory was even larger than the marketplace — endless rooms and courts stacked with bows and arrows, round leather shields, oblong shields of layered cotton made to cover most of the body, rows of clubs and stone-tipped lances.

Though tempted, I said nothing about the powder I had stored away, one keg of which could reduce the armory to a pile of rubble. Nor did I mention the muskets, which could mow down ranks of bowmen like so many rows of corn. Nor did I speak of the cannon, which could topple their highest pyramid.

I came away with the knowledge that every man in the city was either a warrior or aspired to be one. That any town or city or province that was free and intended to stay free was considered a rebel. That it was their business to make war and other people's business to work and die for them.

I saw the warehouses where the tributes from vassal cities were stored as they were brought in from time to time. I learned how the accounts were kept, what the tributes consisted of and in what quantities.

The province of Xochipilli, for instance, sent the Emperor each year 4,850 loads of women's clothes, 725 loads each of loincloths and skirts, 550 loads of chili peppers, 11,300 bunches of parrot feathers, 10,600 balls of rubber, 15 packets of quetzal plumes, 130 large sheets of agave paper, 360 live birds, and 17 gold bars.

Province by province, city by city, none was exempt from tribute. Those who did not pay or skimped their tax were severely punished — sometimes the people of an entire town would be sold into slavery.

I was shown the archives, which were many times larger than mine, the whole more conveniently arranged and better kept, with sixty artists and writers busy at work.

As we walked away from the archives, I decided to thank the lord for his courtesies and inform him that I was ready to leave the city. I had done what I had set out to do. I had seen all that I had come to see.

I was overwhelmed by Tenochtitlán.

By its temples and squares, canals and causeways. The streets were clean and lighted and alive with color. Trader caravans spread through the empire and beyond, carrying goods to sell, returning loaded with riches. Tribute in all forms poured into the city. The Emperor could call up a hundred thousand warriors with a single blast of a trumpet.

And the flowers! They grew on rooftops. They came in baskets on people's backs, by canoe and barge. People wore them and strewed the streets with them.

And the banners! They flew from house and temple — long streamers as light as air, woven of red macaw feathers, flags of the blue heron, delicate as cobweb, yellow pennons of tanager and toucan. They rode the wind like great bright birds.

"I leave in the morning," I told Lord Tzapotlan.

"But there's much you haven't seen," he objected. "The Emperor's pleasure garden, its pavilions, the fountains that flow night and day, the zoo, which houses strange beasts from sea and jungle and many oddities of nature, the Emperor's treasure room, unrivaled in all the world. There is much you must see."

"Much, I am sure, Lord Tzapotlan. And now that I have seen what a beautiful city it is and how friendly the Aztéca are, I will come back again."

"I trust it will be soon," the lord said. "Meanwhile, since you are the first of the Maya lords to visit Tenochtitlán, the event will be recorded by our best artists. It will be set down in the archives and preserved in precious stone."

Lord Tzapotlan escorted us to our doorway, bowed, and hurried off as if on urgent business, accompanied by his four servants, who ran along beside him, fanning his person with feathered whisks, for now that night was near the plaza swarmed with insects.

From the window the dwarf and I watched him disappear. The two palace guards, or two men in the same yellow-and-black-striped tunics, were standing not far away. When the lamp tender came past, they moved into the shadows.

"It is always better, they say in Seville, to die tomorrow than it is today," said the dwarf, "so let us leave today. Now! It's clear that we are to play a prominent role in the rites of the war god. Chalco arranged for that

137

before he left. He'll not be back. He's on his way to the coast. When he gets there, what will happen? What happens to the *Santa Margarita?* What becomes of our gold?

"The Emperor's guards stand outside our door," I said. "How far would we get before we're caught and trussed up like a pair of chickens?"

"If we stay," the dwarf said, "in four days we'll be climbing the temple steps."

"We know only one way out of the city. The way we came in."

"Fear is a good guide. It finds ways where none existed before. Back of you is a ladder, which I have already investigated. It leads to the roof."

"*Vámonos,* Guillermo. Let us go."

It was dark now. We built up the fire in the brazier to make the guards think that we were settling down for the night.

Climbing the ladder, we found that we could walk on the roof and that it joined other roofs to the east and west. We set off toward the east, but when we reached the third building we came upon a gap too wide to leap. Retracing our steps, we tried the opposite direction, only to find that escape was impossible.

"What do you think?" the dwarf said.

"We'll have to wait until morning," I said, "and slip out when the vendors are on their way to market. The plaza is always crowded at that hour."

The stars glittered. A cold wind came up and whipped around my legs. A small fire was burning not far from our doorway. The palace guards were huddled around it, their clubs lying beside them.

"We go in the morning," the dwarf said.

"Early, señor!"

In the morning, as the plaza filled with vendors and we were ready to leave, Lord Tzapotlan appeared at the door. He wore lordly regalia — a red embroidered tunic and a blue-feathered cloak — but all was askew, as if he had dressed in a hurry.

He spoke calmly, however, of small things, as is the Indian custom, then in a distressed tone said, "The Emperor has had a vision. Perhaps it is not a vision, but a presence. There is a difference. Do you understand what I mean?"

"Yes," I said, thinking in Christian terms, "I do understand."

"Yesterday the vision came," said Tzapotlan. "This is how. The Emperor awakened from his sleep in the afternoon. He lit his pipe and smoked. In the smoke a face began to form — the eyes first, then the nose, then the lips — until it was a face looking at him. Until it was *your* face looking at him."

The young lord glanced at me, his eyes half closed and clouded, as if he had been partaking of *teonanacatl*. This was a black fungus that the Aztéca ate with honey. He had offered me one of these little black buttons the previous day.

"Was the Emperor smoking something that would give him visions?" I asked.

"A few *mixitl* seeds, but not so many that he would see a face. Your face. Yet this is not all. A hunter came from the lake. With him he had a bird that he had caught in his fowling net. The Emperor had never seen a bird like it. It had feathers that grew in circles, like eyes, and the eyes were blue-colored, like yours. But this was not the thing that made the bird so odd. Its eyes were mirrors that showed pictures of the sky and the stars. When the Revered Speaker looked into the bird's eyes he did not see the sky and the stars, only a picture of many men, and they were sitting on the backs of deer, holding spears in their hands and riding fast."

Lord Tzapotlan paused to allow me to speak.

"He saw them clearly," I said. "Armed men riding on the backs of deer?"

"Clearly in the round mirrors of the bird's two eyes."

"What then?"

"Then the Great Speaker was alarmed and he sent for the wisest of his *tomalpouhque*. He said to him, 'Do you see what I have seen? Look and you will find a crowd of people coming.' But before the soothsayer could answer, the bird fluttered its wings and vanished."

I concealed my disbelief as best I could. The dwarf got up and put wood in the brazier.

"We'll never leave the city," he said to me, "except as hummingbirds."

"The Emperor," Tzapotlan said, "is much disturbed by these men who ride on the backs of deer and carry spears. He did not sleep last night for thinking about these things. This morning he called his soothsayers, but they could not help his mind."

"Why do you tell me about the Emperor's distress?"

"Because I believe that you might counsel with him. He looks upon you as a wise young man, as do I, from the questions you asked about our country and the love you show for your own. Besides, it is your face that he saw clearly in the smoke cloud."

Lord Tzapotlan went on. "The thing of the bird is only the latest of many evils that have come to pass. Nine years ago the lake of Téxcoco, for no reason that could be seen, overflowed and furiously swept off many of the buildings in this city. Only a year later, one of the temples of the pyramid mysteriously took fire and no-body could stop it. Then there were three comets in the sky. Then a light broke forth in the east and rose in clouds that tossed red sparks everywhere. The Emperor took counsel with Nezahualpilli, but the royal sage cast even a deeper gloom upon him. He predicted, three times over, that these events foretold the downfall of Tenochtitlán. Its downfall!"

The lord glanced at our few belongings, which were in a roll beside the brazier. He must have smiled to himself, knowing as he did that the Emperor would never allow us to leave the city.

"You have told me your plans," he said, "and I understand them. But you are needed here. Come, my dear friends."

A number of armed servants had appeared with Lord Tzapotlan. One of them opened the door for us to pass.

The dwarf said, "Shall we go or not? I would as soon die here and now as later on the pyramid."

"We say a prayer and go, Guillermo."

The Emperor was finishing his breakfast as we arrived. He sat behind a gold screen so that no one except the servants would see him, and they were removing it as we were ushered in. A servant held out a gold finger-bowl. The Emperor waved it away. He had eaten nothing from the dozens of gold dishes that covered the table.

This chamber, which adjoined the throne room, was less than half its size. The walls were painted with bright scenes and hung with draperies of rich quetzal plumes. Four dwarfs, a hunchback, and a group of musicians huddled in a dim corner, as if the Emperor had banished them from his sight.

We entered the room, not walking directly toward him, but to one side along the wall, as we were instructed. We bowed and touched the floor with our hands and remembered not to look at him.

Moctezuma said nothing for a long time.

His skin was pale and he seemed to be in a trance; his

gaze moved slowly about the room, over the various scenes painted on the walls. On one scene, which depicted him as a young man receiving the jeweled diadem of an emperor, his gaze rested. He looked away at other scenes — some of battles fought and victims slain, others of festivals and flowery meadows — but always his eyes came back to the one that showed him receiving his jeweled crown.

Lord Tzapotlan spoke in a whisper. The Emperor awakened from his trance and motioned to his servants, one of whom disappeared and quickly returned with a roll of sisal cloth.

The Emperor's gaze again drifted away to the various scenes on the walls. Again Lord Tzapotlan whispered to him. The Emperor lowered his eyes and by chance our gazes met. There was fear in his eyes and something more terrible than fear.

Calling the interpreter to his side, he said to me, "Five days ago, perhaps it was six days — I have lost count. It was the day after the hunter brought the bird that had eyes like mirrors and I saw men riding the backs of deer. It was two days before that day the runners came from the coast, from the sea where fish and turtles are caught. They brought news of a strange sight, which from excitement they were unable to describe. Thereupon I sent artists to paint the strange things the runners had seen."

The Emperor was silent for a while, then he roused himself and spoke to the servants.

Two men unloosed the roll they had brought, holding it up between them. On it, painted in true colors, using white for the sand, blue for the sea, black for the caravels, and white for their sails, was a picture of a fleet riding at anchor behind a small island covered with palm trees. A Spanish fleet!

My astonishment was greater than Moctezuma's must have been when the messengers first unrolled the painting before his startled gaze.

The dwarf whispered, "Help us, Blessed Mary of Seville!," which was as close to my thoughts as anything could be.

"What does this mean?" the Emperor said. "What do you see before you?"

"It is a fleet of big canoes," I answered. "I have seen one of these canoes before."

There were eleven ships in the picture, some large, some small, but all of them unmistakably Spanish, even to the Spanish cross on the sails.

"From where do they come, these big canoes?" the Emperor said.

"From a far country, Great Speaker, a country east beyond the sea. Or so I have been told."

"Who are these people?"

"They call themselves Spaniards."

It was a cold morning with a north wind blowing. A pinewood fire was blazing in a pit in the center of the room, but servants brought Moctezuma a feathered blanket and put it around him. He looked cold and fearful.

"Do you have a message from these people?" I said.

"Two have come. One came yesterday and one came

this morning. They were signed by a man whose name cannot be translated."

A servant handed me a letter written in Náhuatl, which I could not read, but at the end of the letter there was a Spanish rubric with many elaborate flourishes that I deciphered as the name of someone who called himself Hernán Cortés.

I had never known anyone called Cortés, though the man most surely would have lived in Seville at some time in his life. The ships that journeyed to the New World were all outfitted in this city and sailed from there.

"What do these two messages say?" I asked.

"They say that the man wishes to come to Tenochtitlán. This is what he said in the first letter. In the second letter he says that he is already on his way to Tenochtitlán."

"Have you answered the letters?"

"The first one only."

"What did you answer?"

"I said that he must not come."

"What else, Great Speaker?"

"I sent him gold. A gold disk in the shape of the sun, twelve spans high. As high as you stand."

"The last thing to give a Spaniard," the dwarf whispered. "It's like giving honey to a hornet."

"These men ride on the backs of deer?" the Emperor asked.

"Not on deer, but on large animals."

"They ride with spears and thunder sticks?"

"Yes, with many weapons when I saw them."

The Emperor was silent. Then he spoke again and his voice now was the voice of a child, not that of an emperor.

"Do you think," he said, "that these are the same men I saw in the eyes of the fowler's bird?"

"Yes, Revered Speaker, the same."

Servants brought a second roll of sisal cloth, which Moctezuma carefully examined. It was a picture of a Spanish officer in helmet and cuirass, surrounded by soldiers, apparently a portrait of Hernán Cortés.

I could feel the Emperor's gaze fixed upon me, comparing me to the men in the picture, the bearded Spaniards, tanned from long exposure to the sun, and short, not much taller than the Maya, small men even in their heavy armor.

He roused himself and turned to Lord Tzapotlan.

"Looking out my window this morning," he said, "I saw the temple of Uitzilopochtli shining brightly in the sun. That is good. Now we must gather many prisoners."

Lord Tzapotlan gave a figure in Náhuatl that I translated as one thousand.

"Gather twice that number!" the Emperor demanded. "Lord Uitzilopochtli will need all of his strength. Now more than ever!"

Moctezuma did not move from his jaguar bench. He sat quietly with hands folded, gazing beyond the chamber, as if his soul had fled to a distant place.

Lord Tzapotlan spoke to him, but he did not answer.

Then the lord called upon the clowns and they tumbled about while musicians played on their flutes. Moctezuma's gaze never changed. At last the golden screen was brought and placed in front of him.

At once the nobles began to argue. The soothsayers, a dozen old men in yellow gowns and pointed hats, joined the argument, which concerned Hernán Cortés and how he should be treated.

The time had come. *Ya!* It was here.

Without delay, taking the dwarf by the hand, I quietly pushed through the excited crowd. Outside the chamber, we ran through the dimly lit passage that led back to the bridge we had crossed a short time before, to stairs that wound downward from the bridge to the canal.

Here we stopped and looked back. There was no sign that we were being followed.

A double canoe festooned with pennons was nosing

up to the wharf, a feathered carpet was spread out, and a lord and his large retinue of servants, musicians, and guards were making ready to come ashore.

We waited until everyone was on the wharf and drums were beating.

Beyond the canoe was a line of barges tied to stone rings. The canal ran beneath the Emperor's palace and at its far end was a glimmer of sunlight. Judging that the lake lay in that direction, we slipped through the crowd and raced along the wharf toward the end of the tunnel.

We came upon a barge piled high with garbage that was being pushed along by two men with poles. We waited until, having run out of space to walk, they turned about, trotted forward to the bow, and set their poles again.

With Cantú in my arms, I made a leap from the wharf to the moving barge, with good fortune landing on my feet. The two bargemen had not seen us, but they were toiling slowly along the deck. We could either grapple with them or try to hide.

We clawed into the garbage, dug away until we reached bottom. We pulled the rank stuff over us, lay quiet, and waited. Bent over their long poles, grunting as they came, the two men reached the stern, turned around, and went forward to start poling again.

The barge moved into the sunlight. The air freshened.

Peering out through a hole I had left myself, I saw the temple of Uitzilopochtli behind us. To the left was a causeway crowded with people, to the right an expanse of water with white houses beyond and some small temples.

We covered our heads now that we had left the half-light of the tunnel, but the smell grew stronger and I began to cough. There were no sounds from the dwarf. For a while I thought he might be dead. Then he said something that sounded as if he were out of his wits and whispered, "He, he."

We were moving along faster at this time, in water no deeper than my waist. I thought about wading ashore, carrying the dwarf on my back, but we were still too close to the main part of the city.

An hour must have passed, the two Indians tramping back and forth with their long poles, when one of them, a squat young man dressed in a breechclout, hesitated as he reached the stern, fell to his knees less than an arm's length away, then looked squarely at me, blinking his eyes in surprise.

Lacking any choice, I squirmed out of the garbage, picked up the startled Indian, who was half my size, and threw him overboard. The second Indian turned back when he heard the splash, and as he reached me I wrestled him along the deck and finally into the lake.

With the poles we went on for half a league and guided the scow ashore. We washed ourselves, which took a long time, and, finding that we had been this road before, found the causeway that led on to Chololan.

Fires burned in the courtyards we passed, but few people were on the road. We traveled until it was too dark to see, then found a place to sleep.

It was near a hut where a woman was selling maize cakes, but I had nothing to pay for food except the one pearl left from the hoard I had started with. Since we would be traveling in the guise of *pochtéca,* and needed merchandise and decent clothes, we could not part with it. We slept, therefore, on empty stomachs.

At the marketplace in Ayotzingo I traded the pearl for two sets of rough clothes, including sandals for the dwarf, who had somehow lost his, traveling staffs, and a bundle of trading goods. By noon we were on the road again, walking eastward in bright sunshine toward the town of Amecameca.

We went fast, much faster than when we had been traveling toward Tenochtitlán weeks before.

Fear sped our footsteps. Fear that Lord Tzapotlan had sent his men in search of us. Fear that the men whom the Spaniard Cortés had left behind would venture out and in time happen upon the *Santa Margarita.* Fear of Chalco, who by now must have found his way back to the island.

On the fourth day, as we were leaving a grove of trees, there were rapid steps behind us. We hid in the bushes until two youths passed by. I recognized them by their blue headbands as the Emperor's runners.

Not long afterward, another pair passed us going in the opposite direction. I tried to stop them, thinking that they might be carrying news about Hernán Cortés, but with a wave of their hands, they sped on.

People we talked to in Amecameca when we stopped to buy food recognized us.

Children, attracted by the giant and the dwarf, gathered around and followed us through the streets, shouting friendly words, entreating us not to leave them. But we went on as rapidly as Cantú's short legs would permit — some five leagues each day, traveling from dawn to nightfall — with me worried that he would collapse on the trail, unable to take another step.

When we came to the high country between the snowy peaks of Iztaccihuatl and Popocatepetl, we suffered from the cold and could only travel at midday, when the sun was warm.

One morning, halfway through the high pass, the dwarf could not get to his feet. Fortunately, there was a village nearby where I located two strong young men who agreed to carry him in a litter.

We traveled faster now. And since we were leaving the cold peaks behind and the trail trended down, we covered more leagues each day than at any time since we had left Tenochtitlán.

Near the city of Cholólan we came upon four of the runners, who were passing bags to each other on the trail. We stopped, and I asked the two members of the team running westward from the coast if they had heard news of men with beards who were riding on the backs of deer. Both men shook their heads.

In Cholólan I asked a youth if he had heard anything of bearded men carrying sticks that made thunder and spouted fire.

"Tell me more about these men who carry thunder sticks," he said.

"There is much to tell," I said, "but there is no time."

The first we heard of Cortés was when we came to the city of Texcála. Though Cantú was on his feet once more, we had been held back by a *norte,* a freezing wind that covered the land with dust.

151

It was shortly after dawn when we reached Texcála, but torches flamed on the temple steps, drums were beating, and people crowded the streets. I thought that it must be a festival day. Before we had gone far, however, we discovered that the city was under siege.

Hernán Cortés and his army stood at the gates.

The only road to the sea was blocked by the Spaniards and the Texcaltéca, which made it necessary for us to find a way around the two armies.

We wasted the rest of the day discovering that a trail used by deer hunters skirted the city. It led for a league and more in the opposite direction from the way we had to travel, made a winding loop back through a steep ravine, but at last came out on the trail.

With the armies at our backs we made haste along the road to the sea.

There were signs that farmers had been harvesting their fields when Cortés came by and that the Spaniards had stopped to raid the crops and burn the huts where the Indians lived. There were no farmers in the fields, and the only life I saw was a stray dog that stared at me from behind a tuna bush. The big, black-winged *zopilotes* had begun to gather in the sky.

We had not gone far when I saw a spiral of yellow haze less than a league in front of us. The road was soft from the tramping of feet and horses' hooves. I thought that the wind, which had shifted around and now came from the east, was blowing dust toward us.

The dwarf thought differently. "It's not wind," he said, "or men marching. It's men on horses. And being on horses they are Spaniards."

"I think you're wrong about the horses," I said. "The army has gone by. Days ago, judging from the signs."

"A nest of stragglers. Every army has them."

"One or the other, we should not stay here."

We increased our pace and while we were talking, the clear sound of hooves came to us on a gust of wind. There was a hut close at hand, sitting back in a cornfield. Two other huts nearby had been burned to the ground, but this one was standing.

Like all Indian huts, it had a straw mat for a door. The mat had been torn and was hanging loose. As I pulled it aside, I saw in the back of the hut a man sitting hunched against a wall. Beside him lay a woman and a child. The child was breathing but the woman was dead.

We went in and I fixed the curtain straight. I spoke to the man. He did not answer, though he tried, putting his tongue out and parting his lips.

I glanced through a hole in the mat.

The horsemen had slowed down. They wore helmets and breastplates and carried lances across their saddles. They were laughing about something, then they stopped and one of them pointed to the hut. The same man rode through the field, talking over his shoulder to the other soldiers, who were watching from the trail.

I opened the curtain as he rode up and greeted him in Spanish. "We're Spaniards."

"I can see that you aren't Indians," he replied.

He was a very young man, not much older than I, and had a cut on his chin that had not yet healed. He spoke in the accent of Seville, clipping his words off at the ends.

"Who are you?" he asked, glancing past me at the man and the woman and the child. "Why are you here in all this?"

"We saw the hut," I said. "It's the only one that hasn't been burned. We're looking for water."

"I mean, who are you?"

"My name is Julián Escobar, from Seville in Spain."

"I know Seville's in Spain. You don't need to instruct me." On his breastplate, which had a dent in it, was an officer's insignia. "What are you doing on the road? Where are you going?"

"I'm a *pochtecatl*. I trade goods." I pointed to the bundle lying beside the door. "We're on our way to Tzompantzinco."

"You look like a deserter," the officer said. "We've met a couple since we left Vera Cruz. You must belong with Cortés. Or why are you here?"

The dwarf spoke to me in Maya, but because he spoke the language so poorly, I understood only a single word — *citam*. It meant "wild pig," and I assumed that he was reminding me that I was dealing with one.

154

"And you," the officer said, as if he had not seen the dwarf before. "Who are you and where do you come from and why?"

"Guillermo Cantú," the dwarf said and then repeated what I had already said about myself, adding the information that we were both castaways from a Spanish ship.

The officer, worrying about the cut on his chin, kept touching it with a dirty finger. He stopped as something stirred his memory.

"You are not with the ship that sank with Aguilar?" he asked me.

"Aguilar?" I said cautiously, as if I might or might not know him.

"Gerónimo de Aguilar," the officer prompted me. "He was from Ecija in Spain and was cast away in Yucatán three years ago. He's been living with the Indians. Now he's with Cortés as an interpreter."

"I don't know Gerónimo de Aguilar. My friend and I are castaways."

The officer turned his horse and rode back to his six companions and talked for a while. I couldn't hear their conversation, but from their gestures all of them were in favor of letting us go on our way. I expected that the officer would give us a wave and ride on. Instead he rode back to the hut and said that he was taking us to Texcála.

"The Royal Notary has a listing of all our men," he said. "I want to see if he has your names."

"We're not on the Notary's list."

"No doubt, but I'll make certain."

The man who was hunched against the wall of the hut made a motion of his hands, asking for water.

"What are we going to do with this man and his sick child and his dead wife?" I said.

"Leave them," the officer said.

"Do you have water?" I asked.

The officer signaled to the men on the road and one of them came with a gourd, which he gave to the man. Then the officer rode back to his comrades.

The dwarf and I buried the woman. The earth was hard and we had nothing to dig with, so we put her in a shallow place and covered her with cornstalks. I said a prayer for her and took the child in my arms.

The man had gotten to his feet and the four of us went out through the field and started up the trail to Texcála.

"We are in trouble," the dwarf said.

We arrived at the Spanish camp in midafternoon and within a few minutes the dwarf and I proved that we were not and never had been soldiers in Cortés' army. This freed us from one problem, but plunged us into another far worse.

In a brief ceremony, we were pledged to the service of His Majesty King Carlos the Fifth. The dwarf was set to scouring pots in a nearby stream, while I was given a sword and assigned to guard duty on a wind-swept hill.

The hill, less than a league from the outskirts of Texcála, commanded a view of all the approaches to the beleaguered city. Scattered over its crest were numerous fires around which small groups huddled against the wind. Sidling up to one of the fires, I found myself in the company of two ragged soldiers, both with wounds, both surly, whose names were Juan Borrego and Raul Carrasco.

They were silent young men, but I managed to pry out of them answers to the two questions that had plagued me since the moment I first heard of Cortés. I learned that the Spanish fleet had sailed from Havana directly westward to the mainland.

"Did you pass any islands on the voyage?" I asked them.

"Water only," said Juan Borrego. "Lots of water."

"Beautiful blue water," Raul Carrasco added, "but many bad currents and no islands."

"Did you sight any ships?" I asked.

They both agreed that no ships were sighted.

"On the sea or after you landed?"

"When the Captain-General raised the cross and founded the village of Vera Cruz, they came from everywhere by the hundreds."

"But no caravels, then or later."

"None," Carrasco said.

This settled my mind somewhat, but it did not mean that the men who were left to guard the fleet would not take it upon themselves to explore the coast and by chance find the *Santa Margarita*.

"How many ships were in the fleet?" I asked, to confirm the truth of Moctezuma's painting.

"Eleven," Raul Carrasco said. "But now there's none left. Cortés destroyed them all."

"All but one," Juan Borrego corrected him.

"That's a strange thing," I said, thinking that they

157

must be either telling a lie or joking. "I never heard of a captain destroying his own ships."

"He destroyed them," Carrasco repeated. " 'Let all those who lose courage,' he said, 'and wish to leave the expedition, let them have fair warning that their fates are sealed. Turn your backs upon home, for you shall not see it again until we are victorious.' This is what he told us, standing by the cross."

If this were not a lie, if it were true that Cortés had sunk nearly all his fleet, then there was no need for me to worry about anyone finding the *Santa Margarita*.

"To sink ten ships," I said, "almost his entire fleet, this Cortés must think that he has set off on a dangerous campaign."

"Yes," said Carrasco, "and there are many who think likewise. Before us is an army of fifty thousand savages, some say more. And beyond is this Indian king who has ten times that many ready and waiting to cut off our heads."

"Cortés has plans to capture the big Aztéca city, Tenochtitlán?" I asked.

"That's where we're going," Carrasco said, "to the big Indian city."

"That's where you'll find the gold," Juan Borrego said.

"The doorknobs are made of gold," Carrasco said. "Imagine!"

They reminded me of Baltasar Guzmán talking to the crew of the *Santa Margarita* before we reached Isla del Oro, describing to the men how the house of Lope Luzir had doors and walls fashioned of gold.

They were not interested in who I was or where I had come from, only in the dream that had brought them more than two thousand leagues to this cold hillside, in sight of an enemy who vastly outnumbered them, in the province of the mighty Moctezuma, whose gods thirsted for their blood.

•

∽

After a long hour during which we sat in glum silence around the fire, a musket shot rang out. It was a warning and it brought us scrambling to our feet.

A party of Indians was moving along at the bottom of the hill, through a tuna grove. I counted forty, some in the black garb of warriors, others in blue and white robes, led by a masked cacique who reclined on a litter prettily decked out with flowers.

They came slowly to the thud of wooden drums, stopped halfway up the hill, and announced their presence by the screech of many trumpets.

At a walk, as if they did not wish to appear in a hurry, four Spanish horsemen rode past and down the hill to where the Indians were waiting. From the picture Moctezuma had shown me, I recognized one of the Spaniards, a man not much older than thirty, pale of

159

countenance and stiff-backed, holding a tight rein with small, gloved hands, as the conquistador and Captain-General, Hernán Cortés.

The Indians, we learned from word passed up the hill, had come with an offer of peace.

"We've been waiting on the alert now for two days," Juan Borrego said, "not knowing if they will attack us or not. We sleep in our clothes."

"The savages carry swords twice as long as my arm," Raul Carrasco said. "They're made of wood but they have stone teeth that cut deeper than steel."

"With one blow they kill a horse," Juan Borrego said.

"And did," his friend added. "When we were fighting in a village near Cingapacinga, they killed one of our mares, cut her head off with a single blow."

"I hope they're here to make peace," Juan Borrego said.

"This I doubt," Raul Carrasco said. "More likely it's a ruse."

Cortés and the cacique talked for a while, then the assemblage moved up the hill and gathered again not far from us. It seemed as if Cortés, not trusting the Texcaltéca, wished to surround himself with his own soldiers.

The Texcaltéca, it developed, had come with word from their chieftain to say that in his heart he had only peaceful thoughts. As proof, he was sending now Indians with gifts of fowl, bread, fruit, many parrot feathers, and four miserable-looking old women.

The Indians burned copal incense in front of Cortés

and delivered the cacique's message, which, as I over-heard it, contained these words:

"All this is sent you by the Captain Xicoténca so that you may eat. If you are savages, as some say, and wish for a sacrifice, take these four old women, sacrifice them, and consume their flesh and hearts. But as we do not know in what way you do this act, we do not sacrifice them here before you. If you are men, however, eat these fowls and bread and fruit, and if you are not *teules*, devils, make your sacrifice with copal and parrots' feathers."

Cortés heard the message, spoken and then translated, with great impatience. Even his gelding was impatient and kept moving about in circles, the silver bell on its bit tinkling merrily.

Cortés answered that he had not come to make war, that he came in the name of the Lord Jesus Christ and Emperor Carlos. He thanked them for the food they had brought and warned them not to commit any foolishness, but to make peace.

As he talked, an officer rode up and gave him a message. There was something about the rider's drawling words and the way he sat stiffly in the saddle, as stiff-backed and arrogant as Cortés himself, that stirred my memory. But it was the horse he rode that I recognized.

God being my judge, there before me on the windy hillside stood the black stallion, Bravo. And on his back, with his big-roweled Spanish spurs glittering, sat Don Luis de Arroyo.

When I told the dwarf at supper that Don Luis was an

161

officer in Cortés' army and I had seen him in camp, he laughed.

"You're having visions like the Emperor Moctezuma. Either that or in our absence Don Luis has been sacrificed and his heartless ghost has come back to haunt us."

The next morning Don Luis rode down the hill past my watch fire, and I called out to him. He glanced back over his shoulder but without recognizing me — there was no reason why he should, since I wore a helmet several sizes too small and a breastplate that belonged to someone half my girth. He rode on.

I had not gotten over my surprise that he had escaped from his cage, found his way into Cortés' army, and was riding around the camp on my black stallion.

This surprise was small in light of the surprise that awaited me.

Xicoténca had sent Cortés gifts of food and parrot feathers and old women as an act of friendship. It was thought, however, that all his Indians were *quimíchime,* mice, spies who came only to size up weapons, learn how many soldiers Cortés commanded, and find the ways into and out of the camp.

One of these Indians was an old man who toiled up the hill leaning on a stick and asked if he could talk to the chieftain who rode around on a big gray deer. He was dressed in rags, but, thinking that he might carry an important message, I led him to the top of the hill where Cortés had pitched his tent.

Cortés was talking to a comely young woman whom I had caught distant glances of before. She was dressed in a leather skirt and blouse that were remade from an officer's uniform, wore fawn-colored sandals laced to the knees, and had her hair bound in a yellow-and-black neckerchief.

Her name, I had heard, was Doña Marina, and she was Cortés' interpreter, translating Maya and Náhuatl into Spanish.

I led the old man up to Cortés. I was about to leave discreetly, when I caught the girl's eye. She dropped her gaze and quickly turned away, yet in that brief instant, to my great surprise, I saw that the Captain-General's interpreter, Doña Marina, was not a stranger but my friend Ceela Yaxche.

I waited, thinking that I would have a chance to talk to her when Cortés was through with the old man. Why had she left the Island of the Seven Serpents? Had she left with Don Luis? How had she met Cortés and why had she followed him to this place?

I had no chance to ask these questions, for as soon as Doña Marina had translated the old man's message, she hurried off.

The man brought word that Xicoténca was planning to attack the camp by night, choosing that hour because the Spaniards believed that Indians never fought after the sun went down. As soon as Cortés heard the news, he had one of the Texcaltéca seized and taken into the hut where Doña Marina had fled.

I heard talking between Cortés and the Indian, several quiet moans, then the men came out and Cortés called upon two of his officers.

163

"The Texcaltéca who are standing there gaping at me are spies," he said. "Line them against the wall and attend to them."

The officers went about collecting the Indians — there were seventeen standing about — and herded them against the wall. Then two of the officers, wielding swords, stepped quickly down the line. They hacked off the hands of the first man, the thumbs of the next, the hands of the third, and so on.

When the officers were finished, Cortés said to the Texcaltéca, "Go and tell Xicoténca that this is punishment for his audacity. Tell him also that if he wishes to come, for him to come any time, day or night. And if he does not come, I, Hernán Cortés, will seek him out in his own house."

By some mistake the old man had been lined up with the rest. Fortunately, he did not lose his hands, only his thumbs.

He picked up his cane and went down the trail, a slow step at a time. The rest of the men fled in terror, clasping their arms across their breasts.

Cortés and his officers began talking again. I stood there staring at them in disbelief until one of the officers with an oath ordered me back to my watch.

Toward noon of the following day, while I sat huddled half-frozen over the hillside fire, I looked up to see Don Luis riding along the trail, erect in the saddle, his legs hanging free.

As I stood up, he swung down from the saddle and grasped me in a tight *embrazo*.

"I caught a glimpse of you yesterday," Don Luis said,

"but I was busy with the Indians — a stupid lot."

He paused to embrace me a second time. Stepping back, he glanced at my ill-fitting armor and the dented steel helmet that sat on top of my head.

"How the gods have fallen," he said. "But perhaps you'll rise again somewhere, perhaps in another life, among the saints."

"You, señor, have risen already," I said. "When seen last, you were dressed in remnants, had a broom in your hand, and on your face a very sour expression."

He did look more like himself — the jaunty nobleman for whom the world was a peach to be plucked. But events had put a bitter look in his eye and a long, white scar across his forehead.

"When I saw you yesterday, Don Luis, I thought you were an apparition."

He smiled, the quick, charming smile that meant nothing. "In that case, if you saw an apparition, you must have thought me quite dead."

I was silent, still unable to believe that the man stood before me, not two paces away.

"You must have given orders for me to die," he said.

"Not exactly. But tell me how you didn't."

Don Luis fingered his sword, groping for words. "I've no intention of revealing how I escaped," he said. "I may wish to do so again."

"You're riding Bravo. I recognized him at once, though he's in bad need of grooming, walks with a limp, and somebody has bobbed his tail."

"An Otomí did it last week. I got even by bobbing the Indian's head."

165

"You had help to get yourself out of jail, steal the horse from the palace, and then cross to the mainland. Who was it? Cortés?"

"No, he hasn't been near the island. But he will be, and soon if his campaign against Moctezuma succeeds."

"It can't succeed. Moctezuma has an army of a hundred thousand wild soldiers, ready and anxious to fight. What does Cortés have?"

"Four hundred men or less, all of them worn out and many sick. A thousand Indians armed with clubs."

There was a watch fire near us with men sitting around it. Don Luis turned his back on them and lowered his voice.

"The campaign has been foolish from the start," he said. "Every day that goes by proves it. We wait now to see if the Indians attack, if we'll be alive tomorrow or not. In the last weeks I haven't had my clothes off. I've slept on the ground with a saddle for a pillow. And I was wounded — you may have noticed the scar — given up for dead. I *would* be dead, except for our surgeon. He had a fat Indian killed and made bandages of the fat and thus saved my life."

My comrades of the previous afternoon came up and sat down by the fire.

"I see by your faces that you are not in a happy mood," Don Luis said to them. "What troubles you?"

"Everything," Juan Borrego answered.

"You would like to go back to Havana?"

"Anywhere," Raul Carrasco said. "To Vera Cruz. Anywhere."

Motioning me to follow, Don Luis walked over and

166

mounted Bravo. "There are two factions in this army," he said. "The *encomenderos,* who like myself own islands in the Indies. The other faction is a gang of adventurers who have nothing to lose."

The stallion pawed the ground. Don Luis glanced down at me from the saddle. There was the look in his eyes, the mad look I had first seen that morning more than a year before, when he had rousted me out of sleep with the tip of his sword, the same look I had seen many times since.

"Join us," he said. "We'll put an end to this Cortés and his vaulting ideas. Imagine a man who scuttles almost all of his ships, turns his back upon any chance of escape, and marches away with a motley band of four hundred to conquer an empire! Neither the Romans nor the great Alexander, nor any of the famous captains ever dared to destroy their ships and brashly set off to attack vast populations and huge armies. Join us, Julián Escobar. You have a ship hidden somewhere along the coast. Let's make for it. I'll gather the *encomenderos* tomorrow and we'll slip away while Cortés is occupied with Xicoténca."

"Give me a little time," I said.

"I'll see that you talk to the other *encomenderos.* There are three of them — all officers and stout men. In addition, we have fifty, at least fifty, common soldiers who are anxious to go with us."

I had no intention of joining him and his renegades, but I needed to delay an answer until the army was farther along the road to Tenochtitlán, at a place where it would be too late for Don Luis to turn back.

If I were to set off with him now I would never reach the coast alive — or alive, I would find myself bound hand and foot, sprawled out on the deck of the *Santa Margarita.*

Don Luis rode off with a wave of his hand, astride my handsome black stallion. I watched him go, unable to lift a finger to prevent it — I, the Lord Kukulcán, afoot on a windswept hill, beside a fire that gave off no heat.

In a fit of anger and frustration, I sent after him a long, bitter curse.

•
•

We need not have feared an attack from Xicoténca.

Upon the return of his spies, seeing that some had lost their thumbs, some their hands, he decided to oppose Cortés no longer and sent messengers to welcome him into the city.

I had given up all thought of escape.

We were surrounded by hostile Texcaltéca, who, though they were afraid of Cortés, would not be afraid of two fleeing soldiers. Furthermore, the dwarf was not able to travel more than half a league without stopping for a long rest.

With me in armor half my size that had belonged to a soldier now dead, and the dwarf carrying five silver dishes from which Cortés ate his meals, we entered the city of Texcála.

There was little room in the streets or on the rooftops, so many people were eager to see us.

The caciques brought food and drink and cones of sweet-scented roses. Some declared that they would bring their daughters and have the officers accept them as wives. Xicoténca did bring his daughter — a most beautiful girl — and after she was baptized and made a true Christian, Cortés agreed that his favorite, Pedro de Alvarado, could take her as his wife. She was given the title of nobility and was called Doña Luisa.

We were in the city but a few hours when ambassadors from the Emperor Moctezuma appeared with rich presents — jewels to the value of three thousand gold pesos, wrought in various shapes, and two hundred pieces of cloth elegantly worked with feathers and other embellishments.

Among the ambassadors was the Emperor's nephew, Lord Tzapotlan. I caught glimpses of him when he first appeared, but managed to evade him for several days. At last, for our camp was small, we met.

"I am not surprised," he said, "to find you here. When the painting of Hernán Cortés came, I was suspicious. I thought you must some connections with this man. Now I find you in his camp."

He spoke to me in a mild tone that I was inclined to distrust.

"When your uncle," I said, "had the painting of

Cortés shown to me, it was the first time I had heard of this man. Until a few days ago, I had never set eyes on him."

I stopped there and did not show my true feelings — that of all the places in the world Cortés' army was the last place I would have chosen.

"From what is rumored," I said, "you have brought word that the Emperor wishes to see Captain-General Cortés."

"You learned when you were talking to the Great Speaker," Lord Tzapotlan said, "that he was confused about the vision he saw in the bird's eye. He thought in the beginning, in the paintings of Cortés and his big canoes, that Cortés was the god Quetzalcóatl returning to be among us. Our wizards thought different and said that Cortés was an invader bent upon our destruction. Now the Emperor has changed his mind again. Now he believes it is decreed by fate, which the chief soothsayer has read in the stars, that Cortés has come to rule peacefully over the nation of the Aztéca. That is our fate."

When Xicoténca heard that the Emperor now was welcoming Cortés as the rightful owner of the crown, he sneered and told Cortés not to put the least trust in Moctezuma. Standing on the campground before our army, he said to Doña Marina, who translated his words:

"You must not believe in the homage Moctezuma has offered. Or in all the presents he has sent, or in any of his promises, for all of this is treachery. In a single hour the Aztéca will take back everything. They will attack you when you are off your guard. And in fighting them remember to leave no one alive whom you are able to kill — neither the young, lest they should grow up to bear arms, nor the old, lest they should give wise counsel."

Xicoténca was a forceful man, tall with a long, dark face, and he pounded his broad chest as he spoke.

He described the fortifications of Tenochtitlán and the lakes, the depth of water, the causeways that led into the city, and the wooden bridges over each of them. How it was possible to go in and out by boat through the openings and how, when the bridges were raised, an army could be caught between them and so be unable to reach the heart of the city. He also said that the houses were built with flat roofs and provided with parapets, from which their warriors could fight.

All this I knew from my days in Tenochtitlán, but Cortés and his officers had not heard it before.

Soon after this, word got to them, probably from Don Luis, that I had been in Tenochtitlán. Whereupon they queried me and the dwarf. Both of us denied that we knew more than they had learned from Xicoténca. We were confused. We were beset on every side by enemies.

As the dwarf expressed it, "Jonah found himself in the stomach of a gentle whale. Ourselves we find in the stomach of a tiger."

We were sitting beside a scanty fire, for wood was scarce in camp, with a cold moon streaming down upon us.

"I let Don Luis know today that we are not with him and the *encomenderos*. But this won't keep him from deserting before we travel another league. If he does, he and the other rebellious officers and the fifty soldiers will head straight for the coast. I see him raise his sword and smile when his eyes fall on the *Santa Margarita.*"

The dwarf jumped to his feet. "I'll go now," he said, "and make sure that he has other matters to occupy his thoughts. I've never been able to talk to Cortés, but I can talk to Doña Marina."

I had seen little of her since the days before we marched into Texcála. When our paths crossed and it seemed as though we were about to meet face to face, she had disappeared, mysteriously almost, from sight. No doubt she still looked upon me as the god Kukulcán. What she had said to Cortés I had no way of knowing — if, indeed, she had so much as spoken my name.

"You may have trouble with her," I said. "She had some part in getting Don Luis out of his cage."

"Whatever happened," the dwarf said, "now she is loyal only to Hernán Cortés. I imagine she'll be interested to learn what Don Luis thinks about her hero."

An hour after the dwarf talked to Doña Marina, Don Luis was seized, along with three of the rebellious officers. They now were in chains strung from one to the other, on foot and heavily guarded.

After seventeen days, having rested his army, the Captain-General moved on toward the city of Cholólan, taking with him two thousand Indians to carry his baggage and artillery. Also to serve as warriors, for he had been warned by Xicoténca that a turbulent people lived in Cholólan.

We made camp the first night beside a river close to the city. While we were cooking supper, five caciques

172

came to welcome us. They brought gifts of poultry and maize cakes and said that more of their caciques would come in the morning to greet us.

Cortés posted sentries, sent out scouts in all directions, and ordered us to sleep in our clothes. But the night was peaceful.

At dawn we set off and had not gone far when a large group of nobles appeared, followed by a multitude of curious Indians who had heard about our horses and big staghounds and wished to see them.

Their priests carried braziers of sweet copal with which they perfumed Cortés and everyone else around him. It was a very friendly scene until the caciques learned that our army was accompanied by their bitter enemies, the Texcaltéca.

Whereupon three of their chief nobles came forward. Cortés, on his gray gelding, watched with a wary eye. One of the nobles said to him, speaking through Doña Marina:

"Forgive us, noble warrior, for not having come to see you in Texcála to bring you food and presents. It was not for lack of good will but because of our foe, Xicoténca, and his people, who have spoken much evil about us and our lord, Moctezuma. And not satisfied with abusing us they now have grown so bold, under your protection, as to come to our city armed. We beg you to send them back to their country, or at least to tell them to stay outside in the fields. But as for yourselves, you are welcome."

I stood near Cortés during this speech. The man, ruthless and at times evil, driven by something that rendered him fearless, fascinated me. I doubted that the request to send the Texcaltéca away was made because they were enemies. Cortés felt differently.

Moved by what he thought was the fairness of the cacique's request, he sent the Texcaltéca into the fields and at once made efforts to calm the city. But no sooner had he ordered the people to return to their duties, open their markets, and so forth, than word of a plot reached our ears.

An old woman, the wife of a cacique who had fallen out with the city elders, secretly visited Doña Marina, or so I heard, and said to her, "Collect all your belongings and come to the cacique's house now, if you wish to escape with your life. This very night or tomorrow, by the command of Moctezuma, every Spaniard in the city will be killed or captured."

Doña Marina, it seems, had doubts about the old woman's story and asked her, since the plan was so secret, how she had heard about it.

"My husband told me," the woman said. "He is a captain of one of the clans in the city, and as captain he is out at this moment with his command. He is giving them orders to join with Moctezuma's men, twenty thousand of them, who are hidden in the ravines at this moment."

"How long have you known about the plot?" Doña Marina asked.

"For three days," the woman said. "Since Moctezuma sent my husband a gilded drum, and rich cloaks and golden gems to three of the other captains, as a bribe to bring to him at least a hundred of the Spaniards."

"You are certain?" Doña Marina said.

"Certain!" the old woman answered. "Three days ago our caciques started on this. They made long poles with collars and many ropes to hold the Spaniards. They dug holes in the streets and built breastworks on the roofs of the houses. They quietly sent their wives and children out of the city. You must come now or risk your life."

"I'll come later, tonight, not now," Doña Marina said, to put the woman off, fearing that an alarm might be sounded before she could warn Cortés.

She burst in upon the captain while he was talking to one of the caciques and told him what she had learned. The story added weight to rumors he had already heard.

That night he gave orders for the army to gird itself, with horses saddled and cannon primed.

●
● ●

At dawn the army was ready.

The big court in the center of the city had only one gate. Beside this gate Cortés had stationed a phalanx of foot soldiers armed with swords and shields. On three sides of the courtyard stood crossbowmen and musketeers. Ranged along the fourth side were officers on horseback, in position to move quickly whenever they were needed. On the steps of the temple sat twenty cannon.

The dwarf and I were placed — or rather we placed ourselves — at a well in the middle of the court that was protected by low stone walls. We were armed with swords of fine temper but were without shields, since there were not enough to go round. Neither of us had thoughts of taking part in the coming battle. If we were attacked, we would defend ourselves, and that was all.

As the sun rose Cortés summoned all the priests and nobles to the courtyard. They came promptly, laughing and singing, followed by hundreds of happy Indians.

When they were inside the gate and the gate was closed, Cortés appeared on his gray gelding. He was not smiling, but he seemed to be in good spirits. Surrounded by a heavy guard, he faced the assembly.

"For what reason," he said, speaking quietly, "have you prepared long, stout poles with collars and many ropes? And why have you raised barricades in the streets and built breastworks on the roofs of your houses? Why are many companies of warriors lying in wait for us in the ravines close by? I ask these questions, but you do not have to answer. I already know the answer. Although we have come here to treat you like brothers, under the commands of our Lord God and King Carlos, you are treacherously planning to kill us and eat our flesh. Already you have prepared the pots with salt and chili."

When Cortés had finished, Doña Marina translated

his words in a clear voice so that all present would understand. Then Cortés spoke again.

"The King's laws," he said, "decree that the treachery of which you are guilty should not go unpunished."

He then ordered a musket to be fired, which was the signal he had chosen.

Whereupon his musketeers leveled a heavy fire against the Cholólans and the crossbowmen joined in. Some of the Indians tried to breach the narrow gate, but were cut down by the swords.

Driven to the lower part of the court, they made a stand against walls they could not scale. Their stones and arrows flew above our heads and landed among the Spaniards, causing wounds but no deaths.

The dwarf and I, with two other soldiers who had been wounded, were ordered from our enclosure. Then the twenty cannon were trained upon those Indians who still were alive.

The massacre lasted less than two hours.

At the end of that time the Texcaltéca, who were waiting in the fields, arrived. There was no fighting for them to do in the courtyard, but, being bitter foes of Cholólan, they ranged through the city, killing all of the enemy they could find. Severed heads rolled in the streets. Bodies and parts of bodies lay about.

Lord Tzapotlan and the three Aztéca ambassadors who had been sent to parley with Cortés were not in the courtyard when the fighting took place, but later they were in the city and saw people hunted down like rats. I think Cortés intended the slaughter as much to impress them and Moctezuma as to punish the people of Cholólan.

In any event, he called me to his quarters the day after the fighting ended.

"I learn that you have been in Tenochtitlán," he said. "You must know something about that city."

Uncomfortable with his question, I resolved that I would reveal nothing that would encourage or help him in the least to do to Tenochtitlán what he had done to the Indians of Cholólan.

"I know little," I said.

"What is the little you do know?"

"It is a city of many canals."

"And bridges?"

"Many."

"Are they fixed or can they be raised and lowered?"

"I have not seen them raised or lowered."

"There are causeways, I hear."

"Several."

"How can they be described?"

"They are wide and rise up from the water to a good height."

Cortés was standing in the doorway — I never saw him seated, except on a horse — and the sun was shining on him. His long hair had a golden glint but, though he was still a young man, his beard was streaked with gray.

"Have you seen Moctezuma?" he asked me. "I understand that you have. What can you say about him?"

"You know his nephew, Lord Tzapotlan," I said.

"They are alike. I find both of them gentle people."

"How can a man be gentle and at the same time sacrifice thousands on the altars of his devilish temples? I take it that you like this man."

"I like him."

"And he looks favorably on you. By the way, what is your name?"

"Julián Escobar," I said, but the name "god Kukulcán" was on my tongue.

Cortés turned to one of his officers. When he spoke to me again his manner had changed.

"I've decided to send you and your dwarfed friend into Tenochtitlán with a message for the Emperor. I received word from him just an hour ago that he does not wish me to enter his city. Tell him that I have made a journey of thousands of leagues for no other reason than to see him and bring friendly greetings from the most powerful king in the world. Therefore it would be a disappointment to me and an insult to my King to turn back now when I stand on his doorstep."

Cortés yanked his sword out of its scabbard and held it before him as if he were making a vow.

"You've seen what has gone on here in Cholólan? You've seen how I treat acts of treachery?"

I nodded.

"If Moctezuma gives you a message like the one I have just received, if he says that he does not wish me to come to Tenochtitlán, then describe to him what you have witnessed here these last days."

"I will describe it," I said, trying to give my voice an

honest ring, "in all its many details. And I shall go rapidly on a good horse. On Bravo, since I have ridden him before."

I was given the stallion, a decent saddle, and a fine Spanish bit and sent on my way in the early afternoon. The dwarf came alone, riding behind me.

I was anxious to deliver the message Cortés had given me, anxious to tell Moctezuma that a scourge stood at the gates of Tenochtitlán. To warn him that unless he called out his thousands of warriors the city would be destroyed, its streets clogged with dead, like the streets of Cholólan.

As we rode along the causeway at a slow trot, the memory of the ruined fields and burned huts and the dead woman went with me. I saw again the old man without thumbs stumbling down the hill, the men of Texcála fleeing with their bloody hands clasped to their breasts, the courtyard at Cholólan heavy with smoke and sad with the moans of the dying, the streets where people were hunted down from house to house and heads rolled in the gutters.

It was not these sights, however, that sent me hurrying to Moctezuma's door resolved to help him turn back Hernán Cortés, to annihilate him and his army. Truthfully, I must confess, it was the thought of the death and devastation that this Spanish monster might inflict upon my island.

•

• • •

We arrived in Tenochtitlán to find torches flaming everywhere along the causeway, the plaza strewn with flowers and filled with a curious throng, word having reached the city of the beast with a voice like thunder that ran much faster than a deer and carried a man on its back.

Indeed, so curious were the Indians that as they lost their fears, they began to press around us and had to be driven away. So keen was their delight, I regretted that the stallion had only a small part of his once magnificent tail to show them.

Lord Tzapotlan led us to the Emperor's palace, I still riding Bravo and the dwarf clinging on behind. A place for the stallion was waiting, and for us a series of rooms, sparsely furnished but with braziers burning and flowers scattered about.

Lord Tzapotlan had water brought to us in silver bowls and then disappeared, saying that he would see the Revered Speaker and arrange for our meeting. I thought because of the important message I carried that the Emperor would be anxious to see us. But Lord Tzapotlan came back in a short time with distressing news.

"The Great Emperor," he said, "has locked himself away. He is taking neither food nor drink. He has only Tenayuca, his trusted soothsayer, at his side."

"You understand the urgent message I carry from Captain-General Cortés?"

"It is understood," the lord said. "I spoke of it to the wizard."

"The Emperor won't talk to you?"

"He'll talk to no one except to Tenayuca."

We waited that night with no word from Lord Tzapotlan. But in the morning one of the servants said that she had heard that the Emperor had left the palace secretly during the night and gone to the temple of Uitzilopochtli, where he had prayed for a sign from the war god.

The Emperor remained in the temple for two days, praying and burning incense, surrounded by wizards.

On the third day at noon, Lord Tzapotlan came and led me to a chamber different from the one I had visited before. The walls and ceiling were bare and painted a pearly white, which gave me a feeling that I was suspended in the sky, floating high among drifting clouds.

Moctezuma was sitting on a mat that was the same color as the walls, woven of dovelike feathers. I stood before him in my bare feet, out of respect, and gave him the message that Cortés had given me, only softening it somewhat from the harsh words Cortés had angrily spoken.

A confused man, thin and visibly different from the proud emperor I had once talked to, sat before me. He seemed even more confused than on the morning he had shown me the painting of the Spanish ships.

A servant brought forth a long-stemmed reed packed with a brown substance, which he had lit. The Emperor put the stem in his mouth and sucked on it. Smoke came out from his nostrils. He did this but once, then put it aside, as if it were suddenly distasteful.

"Tell me," he said, "you of the sunlit hair, with whom I hoped to talk during many hours, to whom I wished to make princely gifts, who fled from me not knowing that I planned for you the most exalted of deaths, tell me . . ."

Moctezuma paused. I began to wonder if he had lost the thread of his thought or if he had changed his mind about what he had started to say.

"Tell me," he said, moving his gaze from the dove-colored walls that seemed to drift about like clouds, "tell me, why did you flee?"

"Truly," I said in a firm voice, "I fled because I did not want to die on the altar stone."

"But when we talked before, you agreed that it was a great honor to die and be transported to a warrior's heaven, the place of flowers and hummingbirds and life everlasting."

"I discovered, thinking about it later, that I was not yet ready to visit this place of hummingbirds and flowers. I have more battles to fight, many more prisoners to take."

At that moment, looking at the Emperor's gold-shod feet, I saw them move nervously back and forth. I took from this that my answer had diminished me in his eyes. He was silent for a long time.

"I showed you," he said at last, "the pictures my artists painted of Cortés and his captains. They do not look like you, but still they have an air about them, all these men who call themselves Spaniards, that I find about you. Are you one of them? Are you a Spaniard?"

I nodded.

"A Spaniard in the army of this Cortés?"

"No, I am a seminarian. Someday I hope to be a priest. I was cast away on an island off the coast, among the Maya."

"I have heard of a white man who was left on this coast. He became a great cacique."

"The man you name is Gerónimo de Aguilar."

"You are not a spy for this Cortés?" the Emperor said.

"No."

"You have seen Cortés. You have talked to him. You have brought a message from Cortés. You were with him, so my ambassadors say, in Texcála and Cholólan. What do you think of this Hernán Cortés?"

I had no difficulty in answering this question.

"He is a ruthless man, cruel and ambitious and without fear of anything or anyone, even you, Revered Speaker."

"He says, he has said many times, since the day he left the sea, that he comes to visit a city about which he has heard marvelous things and to pledge me loyalty and . . ."

"The loyalty is only to himself," I broke in.

"To pledge loyalty and to inform me about his king and his god. Lately, in a message sent from Texcála, he scolds me about the Aztéca gods and our rites. We have worshipped our gods from the long beginning. In our own way. And we know them to be good. Your gods may be good, also. Is this why he wishes to come, to scold me again?"

"It is not why he comes," I said. "He comes as a conqueror to subdue the city, to kill all those who seek to defend it, to kill you yourself should you dare to oppose him."

Moctezuma showed no emotion at these words. He turned his gaze to the wall, to the stars I had not noticed before painted there among the clouds, and fell silent.

I left with the strong belief that he would oppose Cortés' entry into the city and that Lord Tzapotlan, who had heard of the happening in Texcála and himself had seen the carnage in Cholólan, would stand firmly behind him.

My belief, however, was not borne out.

No sooner had Cortés appeared on the outskirts of the city than the Emperor went forth to greet him, carrying presents of gold. With the Emperor were Cacámatzin, Revered Speaker of Texcóco, the lord of Tlácopan, and a company of Arrow, Eagle, and Jaguar Knights, bedecked in feathers and jade insignias, who swept the causeway clean and scattered it with flowers as the Captain-General advanced.

The lords supported Moctezuma upon a litter, beneath a rich canopy of green feathers, and when Cortés was close at hand he descended and walked on bare feet to meet him. A number of lords went ahead, sweeping his path, laying cloaks so that his feet would not touch the earth.

185

Upon seeing the Emperor, Cortés jumped from his horse. When the two came close, each bowed to the other. Moctezuma welcomed Cortés and he, speaking through Doña Marina, who stood at his side proudly holding aloft his personal banner, wished the Emperor good health.

Cortés then brought out a necklace of colored glass, dipped in musk to give it a pleasant odor, and hung it around the Emperor's neck.

As he did so, Cortés attempted to take hold of him in a hearty Spanish *embrazo*. But the lords who stood around Moctezuma quickly grasped Cortés' arms, for they felt that this was an indignity.

Afterward, Hernán Cortés made another complimentary speech, thanking Moctezuma for being there to greet him, and saying that it rejoiced his heart to meet the great Emperor. Whereupon Moctezuma ordered his nephew, the lord of Texcóco, to accompany Cortés and his captains into the city.

They were escorted to a large house located on the plaza close to the royal palace.

Taking Cortés by the hand, Moctezuma led him to a richly furnished hall where the captain was to stay, gave him a heavy necklace fashioned of golden crabs, and disappeared, suggesting that he rest from his hard journey.

Cortés waited until the Emperor's entourage was out of earshot, then called me over and queried me at length.

"The Emperor seems friendly," he said. "Perhaps a

shade too friendly. Is he sincere in his protestations? The Indians are good at this game of deceit."

As are you, I thought.

"What do you make of him?" Cortés asked.

"He's confused," I said.

"I gather this from his messages, which changed from week to week, lately from day to day. If I had waited for him to make up his mind I would still be camped in Chololán. But now that I am inside the gates, what can we expect? Will he strangle us in the night while we sleep — or gather our men for a festival, then treacherously fall upon them?"

As you did with the men and women of Chololán, I wanted to say.

"The Emperor has a vast army," I said. "He should be treated with respect."

"I intend to, but I am not here to trade compliments and gifts. Remember this when you talk to him. And do so at once. He seems to put trust in you. Remind him that we come here in the name of God and our King. And do not forget, I have allies, an army of five thousand Texcaltéca camped in the hills. In the meantime, I trust him with all my heart."

There was no truth in the words of Hernán Cortés.

In no respect did he trust the Emperor. He had already given orders to have his army lodged conveniently around the main square, his cannon mounted on the rooftops that commanded the square, and had ordered each soldier to be on the alert.

Why should I go to Moctezuma and repeat the lie that Cortés trusted him with all his heart? I had talked to the Emperor only the day before, recounted the horrors of Cholólan and Texcála, and gravely warned him that a like fate cast its shadow on him. In the face of this he had gone to greet Cortés on bare feet, as an act of humility.

The moment I left the Captain-General's presence I set out to find Doña Marina.

Aware that he held her in the highest esteem, both as an interpreter and as a woman, I knew that she would have influence with Cortés. What would it be, what would I ask of her? I had only the hope that somehow she could prevail upon him to discharge me from the army and send me on my way, out of the land of the Aztéca.

I found her, after a morning's search, in the Emperor's garden on the back of the stallion, Bravo. She was resting the horse but sitting erect in the saddle, as if anxious to gallop off again. There was the same wild look about her that I remembered from long ago, when she had first ridden him in the meadow.

I came upon her unawares and seized the bridle before she had a chance to set spurs to the stallion. She held a whip in her hand and was about to use it upon the intruder before, looking down from the saddle, she recognized me.

There was a moment of silence while she gasped for her breath. Then she moaned and slid from the saddle, glancing about in terror.

She could neither turn and flee through the cypress grove at her back, for it was impenetrable, nor pass me, because I barred her way.

Slowly she sank upon her knees and kissed the earth at my feet. She crouched there, her eyes cast down, muttering, "Oh, Lord of the Evening Star, Lord of Light."

"Doña Marina," I said, using her Spanish name, for I was certain that she was proud of it, "I want you to listen. I talk to you now not as the god Kukulcán, but in a different guise, out of the mouth of the young man you knew on the headland and the cove, the one you brought food and fire."

She started to glance up at me, but, catching herself in time, lowered her eyes. She had long eyelashes and they cast shadows on her cheeks. Her strong hands, clasped together, rested at my feet.

189

"It is necessary for me to leave the city of Tenoch-titlán," I said, "and return to our island. You are to help me. You are to go to the Captain-General and ask him to give me safe passage out of the city. I must leave to-morrow. In two days at the most."

I held the reins for her. She took them and staggered to her feet. I lifted her into the saddle. She sat there, making no effort to leave, as if she were caught in a dream.

I was tempted to ask her how Don Luis had freed himself, whether she had had a part in his escape, and how she had met Hernán Cortés. But, knowing that while she was in her trancelike state I could never pry from her an answer to these questions, I kept silent.

"You have not told the Captain-General that I am the god Kukulcán. You are not to tell him now," I finally cautioned her. "Say that I am a merchant, when you give him my petition. A rich merchant whose favor it is wise for him to cultivate."

She made no reply. She sat limp in the big saddle, her hands clasped to her breast, and scarcely breathing. I slapped the stallion's flank. Swiftly he bore her away, out of the trees and the Emperor's garden.

The dwarf and I had no preparations to make. Our few belongings were on our backs and stored in a small wicker bag. In my belt I still had one pearl, nothing more.

We waited for two days, never leaving our quarters lest word come from Cortés. On the third day I received a note from the Captain-General himself.

"We have an army of Indians waiting in the hills," he

wrote in his florid hand. "But they are, as you know, not to be counted upon. Our own army numbers less than four hundred. I beg leave to inform you that we cannot spare a single man. When it is possible, and I trust it will be before the year is over, I will see that you are promptly relieved of your duties."

This was a blow.

The dwarf suggested that we leave the city at once, in the same way as before. We talked about it for the rest of the day.

That night we went to the wharf. We found an untended canoe and were about to climb into it when four men seized us — not Cortés' soldiers, but guards belonging to Moctezuma. They marched us to the palace and lodged us there in an alcove adjoining the throne room.

After that I saw the Emperor every day, at either breakfast or supper, depending upon his mood. Cantú and I were not allowed out of the palace, but we were treated courteously and fed choice food from his table.

I think Moctezuma found comfort in talking about Cortés, though I never told him what he wanted to hear. Whether it was a day when he was suspicious of the Captain-General or a day when he fawned upon him, I always said that unless he tied up Hernán Cortés and put him safely away somewhere, he would lose his kingdom and his life.

As for Cortés, he was glad to have me located in the palace. Every day or two he would want to know about Moctezuma's mood, whether he was plotting a surprise, what his nobles and astrologers were saying. I told him nothing that could possibly help him.

During this time, I had a chance to observe how the palace was run, the size of the court, what duties each of the nobles was given, and how each was rewarded, whether in gold or titles. I learned much that I hoped to use someday.

Weeks passed. We lost our sense of time. Twice we tried to escape by way of the canal but were caught and returned to the palace.

Cortés and his men were busy tearing down all the idols they could lay their hands on, erecting crosses, setting up pictures of the Virgin, lecturing the priests, and trying to turn them into Christians — from all I could hear, without the least success.

One evening while I sat with the Emperor, the gold screen between us, listening to him talk about a star he had seen in the sky that gave off clouds of sparkling streamers, Hernán Cortés burst into the room, not bothering to remove his boots, and brushed past the guards. Behind him followed Doña Marina and four of his captains.

Gripping the screen, he launched forth into an angry tirade.

"Lord Moctezuma," he said, "I am astonished that you, a valiant prince who have declared yourself our friend, should have ordered your captains stationed on the coast to take up arms against my Spaniards. I am astonished also at their boldness in robbing towns that are under the protection of our King and master, demanding of them Indian men and women to sacrifice."

Moctezuma said nothing in reply.

"Being so much your friend," Cortés went on, "I ordered my captains to serve you in every possible way. But your majesty has acted in quite the opposite fashion toward us. In the affray at Cholólan your captains and a host of warriors received your express commands to kill us. Because of my great affection for you, I overlooked this. But now your captains and vassals have once more lost all shame and are secretly debating whether you do not again wish to have us killed."

Cortés had been speaking in a loud voice. He now softened his words and stood with his arms folded across his chest. Moctezuma remained silent, but it was plain that he had been deeply wounded.

"However, all you have done will be forgiven," Cortés went on, "provided you now come with us to our quarters. And make no protest. You will be as well served and attended there as here in your own palace. But if you cry out or raise any commotion, you will be killed immediately by these captains of mine, whom I have brought for this sole purpose."

The blood drained from Moctezuma's face. Moments passed before he chose to speak.

"Captain Cortés," he said, "I have never ordered my people to take up arms against you. I will now summon my captains so that the truth shall be known and the guilty punished."

He took from his wrist the sign and seal of Uitzilopochtli, which he never called upon except in matters of the first importance.

"I am not a person to whom such an order should be given," he said. "You are a guest, not the Emperor. I have no wish to leave my palace."

There were several rude remarks from Cortés, silence from Moctezuma, then an interruption by one of the captains, Juan Velásquez.

"What is the use of all these words?" he shouted in a terrifying voice. "Either we take him or we knife him. If we do not look after ourselves we shall be dead."

Doña Marina did not translate this threat, but when asked by the Emperor what Velásquez had shouted, she said, "I advise you to go with them immediately to their quarters and make no outcry. I know that they will treat you honorably as the great prince you are. If you stay here, you will be a dead man."

To this the Emperor replied, "Lord Cortés, I see what you have in mind. But I have a son and two legitimate daughters. Take them as hostages and spare me this disgrace. What will my chieftains say if they see me carried off as a prisoner?"

I stood speechless during all this.

With the Emperor's simple request, given in a quiet, heartbroken tone, I was moved to interrupt the talk and speak in his behalf. The words were on my tongue. Wisely I kept silent, realizing that nothing I could say would have any effect upon Cortés and, worse, could place me under deep suspicion.

There was some further argument, but in the end Moctezuma agreed to go. Cortés became very ingratiating.

"I beg you humbly not to be angry," he said. "Tell your chieftains and your guards that you go freely. You have consulted with your idol Uitzilopochtli and your wizards who advise you to accompany us."

One of the Emperor's fine litters then was brought and he was taken to the Spanish quarters.

Freed by this happening from the Emperor's prison, Cantú and I began at once to plan another escape. I first tried to reach Don Luis de Arroyo, thinking that, since he had managed an escape from the City of the Seven Serpents, he might be of help. But I found him under heavy guard and unable to talk.

We returned to the wharf once more, only to discover that we were being followed by the Emperor's guards. Without telling us why, they took us back to the barracks. We presumed that the Emperor had something to do with this.

I saw Moctezuma many times while he was a captive and he always seemed in good spirits. Surrounded by his musicians and acrobats, attended to by his servants and nobles and wizards, he was wholly resigned to the fate that the stars and many omens had portended.

Cortés treated him courteously and went on with the business of dismantling the temples, to which Moctezuma did not object.

There were others, however, who did object — not only to the destruction of their idols, but also to the reign of an Emperor who they thought had betrayed them.

Anger grew, rumors were hatched and passed about. The causeways were filled with Aztéca warriors anxious to fight. The temple square became unsafe after dark and Spanish cannon were trained upon it night and day.

It was a time of extreme danger. Cantú and I were

forced to give up any thought of making our way to the coast.

In the midst of this danger, word came from Vera Cruz that an Admiral Narváez had landed and, with instructions from the Governor of Hispaniola to arrest Cortés for disobedience, was marching inland toward Tenochtitlán. Cortés left immediately to drive him back into the sea.

While he was gone the storm broke.

For many years the Aztéca nobles had held a feast in the name of their war god, called the perfuming of Uitzilopochtli. They asked permission of Pedro de Alvarado, an officer known for his fighting skills as well as his cruelty, who had been left in command by Cortés, if they could hold the feast again and if Moctezuma could come as an honored guest.

Captain Alvarado replied that the feast could be held but that the Emperor must remain in his quarters.

It was a bright day after a week of clouds. The great pyramid shone white. Braziers and urns burned on all the terraces. Flowers were strewn around the square and displayed from the rooftops.

When we went out at the sound of drums and trumpets, nobles were dancing on the temple steps, dressed in feathered cloaks and masks, tinkling bells on their ankles. The square was crowded with Indians and they sang as the nobles danced, tossing flowers at each other.

At the height of the merriment a small cloud of smoke appeared high up on the pyramid, like a white rose. Then there was a roar from a cannon. It was the signal chosen by Pedro de Alvarado for his garrison to rush out with drawn swords.

Those who were not slain there on the steps were caught on long pikes. Those who escaped to the gates of the wall that enclosed the square were killed by musket fire. Not a noble who had come to sing and dance remained alive. And most of those who had come to watch were torn to shreds by cannon fire.

It was like the scene in Cholólan when blood ran in the gutters and bodies lay everywhere.

●

━━━

Captain-General Cortés returned to find Tenochtitlán in revolt.

Angered by the desolation that met his eyes and by the problems of calming an outraged city, he first upbraided Alvarado for stupidly arousing the Indians and then turned his ire upon Moctezuma, calling him an ungrateful dog. Afterward, with gentle words, he coaxed the Emperor into appearing before his people and asking them to lay down their weapons.

Moctezuma roused himself and in his imperial robes

walked to the battlements. The crowds bowed before him and were quiet as he spoke. Not angrily against the brutal massacre, as they expected, but gently about their duties.

"Why do I see my people carrying weapons against their king?" he said. "Is it that you think me a prisoner? If so, you are mistaken. I am no prisoner. The strangers are my guests. Have you come to drive them from the city? That is unnecessary. They will depart, if you will only open the gates for them. Return to your homes. Lay down your weapons. The white men shall go back to their own land. And all shall be at peace again within the walls of Tenochtitlán."

A murmur of contempt swept through the crowd. A noble shouted, "Base Aztecatl, coward, the white men have made you something fit only to weave and spin."

A second noble raised his javelin and brandished it against the Emperor. At once a cloud of stones fell upon the royal train. One of the stones struck Moctezuma's forehead, knocking him to the ground.

The Emperor was borne away amid cries of remorse from the crowd. But their sorrow quickly turned to anger and the crowd again besieged the palace.

Saddened by this happening, I talked to Moctezuma the next morning. He had refused all remedies, had torn off the bandages as soon as they were applied, and as I came before him was wrapped in a bitter silence.

He had sworn himself to silence and I left without his uttering a word.

Five days later, refusing all Christian comfort, saying,

"I will not at this hour desert the faith of my fathers," the Emperor died.

His death marked the closing hours of our days in Tenochtitlán and sent us back to the Spanish quarters.

To counter the hordes that surged in upon us when the news spread, four engines were built of heavy timber. These towers, which sheltered twenty-four soldiers and provided loopholes for musketeers and crossbowmen, were sent out the day after Moctezuma's death, but were overthrown by a crowd of yelling Indians.

That night Cortés ordered us to make ready.

He called the officers and those of us who had served him personally to the Emperor's treasure room. Using rough scales that had been devised, he appraised each gold anklet, each plate, each cup, statue, and trinket. The Royal Notary was there to supervise the weighing and claim the fifth, *la quinta,* that belonged to King Carlos. The value of the treasure he estimated to be in excess of two million gold pesos.

The scene was one of wild excitement, rivaling the one aboard the *Santa Margarita* when Don Luis divided the treasure he had wrung from the Indians of Isla del Oro. There would have been even more excitement had not the threats of our enemies penetrated the thick walls of the treasure house.

I clearly heard one Indian with a stentorian voice shout, "We will throw your bodies to the tigers, lions, and vipers to gorge upon! From your gold you will take small pleasure because you will be dead. And your friends, the Texcaltéca, we will fatten in cages."

199

Threats did not bother the dwarf. Dazzled by the piles of shining metal, he took his time in selecting a goodly armful — all he could carry, in fact.

It was now a question of when the army should leave and by what route.

Cortés decided to retreat to Texcála and discuss future operations there.

The causeway of Tlacopan was the longest by which to flee the city but, as the most circuitous, the least likely to be guarded. Cortés made the decision to leave at night after listening to a soldier named Botello, whose astrological advice he had taken before.

Since there were three canals to cross on the causeway, a portable bridge was constructed and four hundred Indians and fifty soldiers were selected to carry it. We made no more fighting towers, for they had failed us.

Because of my size, I was placed in the squad that was to transport the bridge and position it whenever it was needed. The dwarf, because of his ability to squeeze himself through small holes, accompanied us.

We left our quarters at midnight.

A thin rain was falling as we crossed the square and took the narrow street that led into the causeway Cortés had chosen.

To our surprise, upon reaching the causeway we saw two sentinels standing guard. At our approach they fled howling into the darkness. Immediately the priests keeping night watch on the summit of the temples sounded their horns, and the war drum in the great pyramid temple of Uitzilopochtli sent forth a series of mournful groans.

To our further discomfort, a deep trench had been dug between the street and the causeway that could be crossed only by the use of the portable bridge. It was quickly brought up and slid into place.

The army came in a tight formation behind us. Cortés rode in the lead with half of his officers and Doña Marina, the rest of the officers bringing up the rear.

Between them came first the cannoneers, then the foot soldiers, armed with harquebuses, muskets, and crossbows. All of us, officers and soldiers alike, including the dwarf and me, had discarded our steel breastplates for the quilted cotton armor of the Mexíca, which was less cumbersome, and more effective against arrows and javelins.

Cortés, in need of all the strength he could muster, had released the rebellious officers from their chains, as well as Don Luis de Arroyo, who was given back the stallion Bravo.

The army passed safely over the bridge without seeing the enemy, though Indians surrounded us on three sides, shouting threats and insults.

The drizzle ceased and a half-moon showed.

On one side was the lake, flat-roofed houses on the other. Beyond the causeway, not twenty paces away, canoes began to appear out of the mist.

The drum in the great pyramid sounded again, sad and drawn-out. Whether it was a signal or not, there was suddenly unloosed upon those of us who were carrying the bridge a shower of stones and flaming arrows.

Two men were injured and we had to abandon them. We moved on through the mist, which was turning again to rain. Ahead of us I heard the rattle of muskets but not the sound of cannon. From rooftops, stones and darts fell upon us, accompanied by insults that I did not understand but whose tone left no doubt that the Indians would not rest until they saw us dead.

We moved slowly, carrying the heavy bridge.

Those in the lead shouted back for us to hurry, that they had come to another breach in the causeway. We passed three soldiers slain by arrows and others lying wounded. Two horses had fallen on the slippery road and were struggling beside the lake.

The farther we advanced, the more dead we encountered, Aztéca and Spaniards alike, lying in our way so that we had to tramp upon their bodies.

We came to the second breach to find the army in disarray, the artillery in a tangle, and the horses neighing and trying to stampede. The breach was wider than our bridge. When we attempted to slide it into the breach, the forward end got fouled against the bank. We lit torches and strained at it, but could not pry it loose.

Don Luis, who had appeared from somewhere and stood watching us, said, not to me but to others, "We should have built two bridges instead of one and of different lengths."

An officer — one of his friends — answered, "We should have remained in Cuba and saved our lives, which we are about to lose." Judging from his voice, I guessed that he and his comrades were ready to flee.

The bridge was left where it lay, and the army clambered over it. But then we came to a third breach.

Here, hundreds of Indians were waiting for us, some massed along the lake shore, others crouching in canoes. The dwarf was knocked down by a stone that bounced off his quilted armor. Breathless, but not wounded, he began to stagger under his heavy burden of gold, so I helped him carry part of it.

The rain grew heavy. Our torches went out. Darts and javelins showered upon us and many soldiers fell. A horse ran past with its mane on fire.

Cannon were brought up. Because of wet powder, not all of them fired, but enough did fire to drive the Indians back on the causeway and silence the canoes pressing in on us from the lake.

By now the breach was half-full of crates, spilled supplies, dead horses, and dead soldiers, so we scrambled as best we could to the far side.

Now that I was no longer burdened by the bridge and the dwarf had a lighter load to carry, I said to him, "We are not fighting *against* the Aztéca. Nor are we fighting *for* Cortés and his Spaniards. We are fighting to save our lives. If we see a chance to escape, let us take it."

The dwarf was too exhausted to answer.

The night wore on, but the chance to escape did not come.

Everything was in confusion.

Cortés, from all I could tell, was somewhere beyond us with his musketmen, lost in gray curtains of rain. Between us heavy cannon boomed from time to time and I heard the whine of a harquebus.

Indians were shooting at us from the lake, moving along beside the causeway in their canoes. We passed a falconet and a gunner sprawled beside it, stripped of his uniform and pierced by arrows. We passed a dead staghound and a wounded Indian who held up his hands, asking for mercy.

I saw a pile of gold bars from a horde that Cortés had melted down, lying on the causeway. They were no larger than a lady's hand, but their owner had found them too heavy to carry. I left them and said nothing to the dwarf.

We were now at the rear of the army, in a dangerous position, stumbling ahead in the dark, soaked to the bones. The rain stopped again and we lit torches, which attracted arrows, but we moved faster and felt in better spirits with the torchlight shining.

Near dawn we reached the end of the causeway. Cortés and his men were still out of sight, but I could hear musket fire and cannon.

After leaving the causeway, we went forward on a road that ran deep with muddy water. We passed cannon mired to their axles and abandoned, more dead horses, and five dead soldiers in a pile. We came to a small, four-sided pyramid that stood just off the road. Here, in the role he had taken over as our captain, Don Luis pulled in his horse.

"We'll wait," he said. "At sunrise we'll count bullets, climb the pyramid, and survey the countryside."

Cantú and I hung back as he tied the stallion.

The dwarf was for leaving him and pressing on. But it was a better idea for us to climb the pyramid and from its height find out, as best we could, if there were Indians hiding around us, where the road led, whether it went in a circle around the lake and back to Tenochtitlán or to the sea, what had happened to Cortés and to the remnants of his army.

●
●
────────

It was near dawn, with the sky gray and a streak of pink mist off to the east, when we went up the pyramid, the dwarf clasping his gold. Of the fifty soldiers who had started from Tenochtitlán, only nine remained. Three of them, too weak to make the steep climb, stayed behind.

There was a godhouse at the summit and a terrace that looked out on the valley we had left. Off to my right I had a clear view of the causeway and the lake on both sides.

In the dim light I could see canoes wrecked on the shores, drowned men floating, and bodies piled up at the last breach we had crossed.

In the other direction, at the end of the road we had just left, were a group of buildings and a tree-lined square. A fire burned in the square, and around it the remnants of the Spanish army were huddling against the cold.

We left Don Luis and the soldiers talking beside the godhouse.

The stairs were slippery with rain. We went down slowly, a step at a time. Halfway to the bottom I heard an owl hoot, an answering sound, then a second hoot, long and drawn out, high above us.

Looking up, I saw that the terrace was crowded with yellow-striped Indians. Apparently they had seen us climb the pyramid and had gone to its far side and waited out of sight. There were more than a dozen of them running around in front of the godhouse. One pointed down at us and brandished a club.

We had no way of defending ourselves if we were attacked. I carried a battered musket and a pouch of wet powder. The dwarf had lost his sword, his only weapon.

I put an arm around him and we hurried as best we could to the bottom. The three soldiers had built themselves a fire and were lying around it. Bravo stood shivering under the tree. I untied him, got into the saddle, and pulled the dwarf up behind me.

It was still dark here below, but the first rays of sun had reached the terrace. The Indians were chanting as they dragged a body toward the godhouse.

The chanting ceased. There was no sound except a cannon shot far in the distance. The silence deepened. I heard a Spanish oath that Don Luis often used, then quickly a single, choked cry. Black-robed priests came out of the godhouse and one of them held up a bloody heart to the rising sun.

"It was a stout heart," the dwarf said.

"Stout," I said.

"If we had time we could stop and bury him."

"If we had a dozen soldiers with muskets and dry powder."

"It would do little good. The Aztéca would dig him up."

The Indians had left the terrace and were clambering down the stairs toward us. Wishing that I had a pair of Spanish spurs, I thrust my heels into the stallion's flank.

The dwarf said, "We might say a prayer for his soul."

"Let's pray for ourselves. Let us think about getting out of the mud and into Cholólan."

The dwarf still puffed and wheezed from the blow on his chest. "A hundred arrows came your way during the night and many stones," he said, "yet not one struck you in all that time. It puzzles me."

He caught his breath and waited for an answer. When I remained silent, he said, "Oh, yes, I forgot that gods, unlike us mortals, don't suffer such misfortunes. He, he, he."

Before we came to the village where Cortés had drawn up, we saw five riderless horses. Three were mares and two were geldings. We tied the mares behind us.

The dwarf clung to me with one arm, holding his bag of gold in the other, until I could bear it no longer and made him tie the bag to one of the mares.

Two staghounds were wandering around without masters, but we could not catch them, and two riderless horses ran from us.

There was not much of an army left. Most of it lay behind, piled up on the causeway or drowned in the shallow waters of the lake.

Through the trees I caught a glimpse of a small fire and Cortés standing by it among a handful of his officers, with Doña Marina at his side in her fawnskin boots and bright red dress. I felt a pang of regret that she would never again see the stallion she loved so much. But the feeling lasted only a moment, for who could say with certainty that she would not.

Cortés had been defeated, his army cut in half, his Indian allies scattered to the hills, where they would lick their wounds and have second thoughts about his invincibility. Yet a man who could burn his ships behind him and boldly hack his way into the heart of the Aztéca empire was not apt to give up at his first defeat.

We circled around the camp, keeping well out of sight, past a cluster of huts that were burning, and rode into Cholólan at noon. We traded one of the gold figures, a statue the size of my thumb, for a bundle of maize cakes, though it hurt Cantú to do so.

The dwarf said, "When do we reach the sea?"

"If we make nine leagues each day," I said, "if all goes well, if the enemies Cortés has made along the way don't attack us, we should reach it short of a week."

"What do you think about our caravel?" the dwarf said. "And the gold she carries?"

"I don't think about them."

"You must think about something."

"I think about all there is to do once we reach home."

The memory of Tenochtitlán before the conquista-

dores began to tear it apart rode with me. I was bringing
back the vision I had gone in search of and found. It
glowed in my mind like a priceless gem, all radiance and
shimmering color.

"There's nothing else you think of?"

"I think about Cortés and how he will either gather
up his army and return to conquer the Aztéca, now that
he's learned a lesson, or perhaps turn his back on them
and strike out for the coast."

"Either way, we'll see him again," the dwarf said.

"Sooner or later."

We avoided Texcála and came to the province of Xocotlán ruled by Ozintec, the young lord with the dyed
red hair. We would have avoided this place also, had we
any choice, but it lay in a steep canyon enclosed by
mountains. There was no way around it.

Ozintec was surprised to see us; no doubt he thought
that we had long since been stretched out on the sacrificial stone. Recalling that struck by our freakish looks
he had tried to buy us from Chalco, I put on a bold
front and said that we were on a mission for Hernán
Cortés.

We were clothed in armor and astride horses, where
my height and the dwarf's short legs were not so notice-
able, yet the lord gave us long, covetous glances.

"Have you seen Chalco the Aztecatl?" I asked. "I
carry an important message for him." I had to repeat the
lie before he answered me.

"Chalco, yes. He passed this way many weeks ago,"
the lord said.

"On his way to the coast?"

"Yes, in that direction."

"Alone?"

"Alone, no. He had for company sixty warriors from the province of Chalca, with many drums and trumpets. Also with many jars of moss."

"*Tecuítcal.*"

Ozintec nodded, pushing back his long red hair. He was still bemused by the sight of the two freaks that Chalco had refused to sell him.

"You must come and eat with me in the palace," he said.

Behind him stood the stone racks I had noticed before, their thousands of bleached skulls neatly arranged in rows. Above them stood a temple whose steps and terraces were brown with dried blood.

"Come," Lord Ozintec said. "I will serve you a feast of swordfish brought fresh from the sea, roasted duck and boiled iguana."

We had ridden hard since dawn, eaten nothing all day except two small cactus apples, and yet I did not hesitate to refuse his invitation.

"We are honored," I said. "It is kind of you to offer food to two exhausted and hungry men, but as I have said, we carry an urgent message from General Cortés to Chalco the High Priest. You have met Cortés? Yes. Then you know why I wish to deliver his message without delay."

"I know," said Ozintec. "I have seen him."

Without further words we turned away and rode down the street, past the temple and Ozintec's palace.

A half-moon came up. By its light we rode long

after dark. We did not stop until we had put a goodly distance between us and Ozintec.

In the morning we started off before sunrise on a winding trail that led downward into the hot lands. On the trail I discovered the footprints of marching men and among them the tracks of two horses, one being ridden and the other led on a short tether. Beside the tracks were the marks of a staghound.

"Chalco and his Aztéca," I said.

"How old are the prints?" the dwarf asked.

"Old," I said.

"We should ride hard," said the dwarf.

And we did, at a fast *pasotrote,* pausing only to snatch our breakfast from the fruit trees we passed.

Gold from Moctezuma's treasury jingled in the saddle pouches on the back of the dappled mare. The Aztéca had a name for gold. They called it *tonatiuh icúitl,* which means excrement of the sun.

The day had turned warm, with a wind gusting up from the hot country. The sun glittered on the two volcanoes, one of them smoking and one crested with snow. To the east, toward the sea, the sky was blue, but with clouds far down on the horizon.

"Should I dismount and ride one of the mares?" the dwarf said. "The one that carries the gold?"

"You're a bad rider, Guillermo. Remain where you are and hold on."

"As you wish, Lord Feathered Serpent, god Kukulcán."

It was good to hear my name once more.

211